Winning a Gunfight

Securing victory ethically, mentally, and
tactically in a gunfight

Foreword by Lt. Col. (retired) Dave Grossman

Tim Rupp

Printed in the U.S.A by Snowfall Press
snowfallpress.com

In Winning a Gunfight *Dr. Rupp instructs those that value peace, liberty, and freedom to be prepared and not fear when evil comes to "kill, steal, and destroy." His use of real life stories and practical applications in the fundamental principles and latest techniques of winning a gun battle inspires and informs, making* Gunfight *a must read. Life is all about preparation!*

—Detective Joseph Dubs
Twenty-eight year veteran Texas Peace Officer

As I read Winning a Gunfight *I was surprised to find a discussion of ballistics included, as this is the one area most agencies fail to cover in training. As a 34-year veteran of law enforcement and the military, I am a strong believer in always returning to the basics in firearms training. That being said, in this book the basics are covered and the difference between qualification and training should jump off the page as one reads through each chapter. Tim, through his sharing of personal experience in lethal and non-lethal encounters, only serves to validate the need for realistic drilling. Training in Reality Based Scenarios and sound tactical movements such as: drawing from the holster; seeking cover and concealment; and incorporating instinctive shooting drills will only increase your survivability in that crucial moment. Recognizing the ethical, mental, and tactical aspects involved in a gunfight, and using that understanding to assess your own personal limits, will allow you to train for victory rather than become a statistic if ever faced with a lethal threat. This entire volume seeks to say in very simple language "Train As You Fight" or "Train TO WIN."*

—Captain (retired) R.M. "Mike" Tacquard
Texas Department of Public Safety-Highway Patrol

Even as a young USAF Security Police Officer, Tim's approach to officer safety and insight into Winning *helped others to engender a career-long mindset and inspiration to go above and beyond in training and preparation for the ultimate event. This book is a culmination of decades of experience and should be a mandatory primer for both military and civilian peace officers.*

—Master Sergeant (retired) Mark McCue
USAF Security Forces

Winning a Gunfight *is a must read for anyone involved in combat training, or who could find themselves in a gunfight. Tim Rupp provides a holistic approach of addressing the body, soul, and spirit. This style is augmented by Tim's varied training, education, and experience gathered over a lifetime. He served in the military, was a street cop involved in a shooting, and worked as an investigator of officer-involved shootings from two perspectives: as a homicide detective; and as an internal affairs investigator. He has also trained numerous law enforcement personnel in physical fitness, firearms and tactics. His service as a senior pastor provides the necessary connection that allows* Winning *to reach beyond the immediate aftermath of a gunfight and into surviving with more than just your physical life.*

—Deputy Chief (retired) Joery Smittick
San Antonio Police Department

Winning a Gunfight *is a well-written account of one man's direct knowledge gained by living through actual police events. I met Tim Rupp 26 years ago while serving in the United States Air Force Security Police Squadron at Brooks AFB, Texas. Tim is a true professional with an outstanding reputation. He is extremely knowledgeable when it comes to police actions and spiritual advice. This book effectively presents the information and explains the ethical, mental, and physical aspects of being able to win a gun battle.*

—Chief Frank Morales,
Hill Country Village, Texas
35 years experience law enforcement experience

Tim Rupp addresses issues that are relevant today. Winning a Gunfight *does not seem like a book a retired military chaplain would endorse. However, Rupp is speaking to us in terms that come natural for him on every level. He is a trained professional who is training us. He is the pastor of an Alliance Church and speaks to the needs of the soul as well as the body. He challenges the very idea of winning. This book is a textbook, a history book, and a book that will, yes, challenge what it means to be a winner in life. I encourage anyone who has faced life and death situations and survived to read this book. It will ask some difficult questions. Did you just survive or did you win? This book may take you deeper than you expected or wanted. You will find it worth the risk.*

—Chaplain (LTC) Bob Collins, US Army, Retired
Denominational Chaplain Endorser for The C&MA
Deployed to Iraq in 1991

Since 1987 Dr. Tim Rupp and I have played, hunted, cried, and prayed with and for one another. But more than that, we also worked side by side as police officers, detectives, and sergeants in the San Antonio Police Department. From the time I met Tim he was a shining example of a Christian whom I wanted to learn from and get to know better. After years of developing a genuine relationship, I consider it a true honor to be called his friend. Besides all of the other aspects of Tim's life where he has been called to be an outstanding leader (Christian witness, pastor of his church, husband, father, grandfather, friend), I also know him to be a passionate teacher and educator. When Tim decides to teach something, it will be well researched and presented. After reading Winning a Gunfight, *Tim has done it again! If you are considering purchasing a concealed handgun license, purchasing a gun for home protection, or entering any profession where you may be required to carry a firearm,* Winning a Gunfight *by Dr. Timothy Rupp should be required reading before you make that life changing decision! Dr. Rupp examines all aspects of what is required to Win the Fight beyond just surviving the encounter; the epilogue is golden.*

—Sergeant Dave Evans
Homicide Unit
San Antonio Police Department

Winning a Gunfight *is a must read for new law enforcement officers and those who decide to carry a firearm for personal protection. This easy to read book informs the reader of the essential aspects of using force—the ethical, mental, and tactical. And most important of all—understanding your own personal limits. Tim has the unique perspective of adding his actual experience as an officer involved in a shooting, a homicide detective, an internal affairs investigator, and a pastor.*

—Detective Sergeant Karl S. Noah
Bonneville County Sheriff's Office

Winning a Gunfight

Securing victory ethically, mentally, and tactically in a gunfight

by Tim Rupp

ISBN: 978-0-692-78088-6
KDP ISBN: 978-1-519-07156-9

Author Contact Info: office@thestrongblueline.org

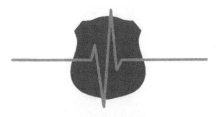

The Strong Blue Line
Idaho Falls, ID
TheStrongBlueLine.org

Winning a Gunfight

Preface

"I am for peace, but when I speak, they are for war!"
the ancient psalmist writes. [1] Men have been fighting (and
killing) each other since the dawn of time; and there's no
indication things will change anytime soon, even as good
men strive for peace. The war between good and evil contin-
ues to rage—even as battles lines are skewed by the people
who insist that all humans are only interested in benevo-
lence, and no one is intentionally seeking to maliciously
harm others.

While good men and women pray for peace and seek
to live in harmony with friends, neighbors, and even their
enemies the fact is, evil remains. No matter what we do, say,
or think, there are some people in this world who are fueled
by a desire to do harm. And given the chance they will kill—
without just cause. Some of these will kill as often and as
much as possible. Others, who are not necessarily bent on
killing, will still resort to it in order to obtain what they want
be it money, drugs, or escape from authority.

Nothing has changed but the weapons. We have
fought with knives, swords, spears, slings, bows, and more
recently guns. As I write this preface the Orlando massacre
of last month is fresh on the minds of Americans and people
around the world. One man armed with modern weapons
murdered 49 people and shot another 53. He was stopped by
good men with guns. The answer isn't to ban guns. The pro-
liferation of mass shootings in America and around the
world isn't due to the proliferation or availability of guns.
We have had semi-automatic rifles in America since the
world wars, yet mass shootings with these rifles are a recent
trend. Guns haven't changed, people have. People who
weren't willing to take up a gun to kill now are willing to do

---

[1] (Psalm 120:7)

i

so. To stop them someone must be willing, prepared, and proficient at fighting. In this case fighting with a gun.

Reading old army manuals, police training material, and books on gunfighting you will read plenty about the mechanics of shooting, cover and concealment, and in more recent resources about tactics. Only recently has the mental aspects of being involved in a gunfight caught the attention of police and military trainers. In the 1990's Lt. Col. Dave Grossman awakened police departments to the critical mental aspects of interpersonal human aggression and the physiological and psychological effects that being involved in a gunfight has on the mind and body (see his books On Killing and On Combat).

In this book I take it one step further and complete the loop. History has shown us that we have worked backwards in preparing for lethal combat. As mentioned, historically the focus was on the skill of using a weapon and the tactics of physically winning. Then we started to address the mental aspects of lethal battle. But where we should begin is with the ethical. Winning a gunfight involves winning at all three levels: the ethical, mental, and physical. Winning a Gunfight will help prepare you to win at all three levels.

Should we seek peace? Absolutely! As a Christian I agree with the biblical mandate, "If possible, so far as it depends on you, live peaceably with all."[2] But, in the event you are not able to live in peace and find yourself in a gunfight are you prepared to win?

Tim Rupp
July 2016

---

[2] (Romans 12:18)

Dedication

To the warriors who have the courage to stand and hold the line between civilization and chaos.

Special thanks to Mrs. Trisha Randall for her editing.

Table of Contents

Preface   i

Dedication   iii

Foreword   vii

Chapters

1. More than Surviving   1

Part One: The Spirit—the Ethical

2. Dealing with Guilt   13

Part Two: The Soul—the Mental

3. Make a Decision!   31

4. Training—for Reality   39

5. The Implications of Being Involved in a Gunfight   49

6. Conditions for Battle   73

7. Real-Life Scenario Training   87

Part Three: The Body—the Tactical

8. Firearms Basics   97

9. Combat Shooting: An Old Way to Shoot Revived   117

10. Equipment   131

11. A Final Word   149

Epilogue   153

Appendix A: FBI Qualification Course   157

Works Cited   161

About the Author   171

Foreword

You hold in your hands an amazing book, unlike any other on the subject. Many good books have been written about this critically important topic, but this is the only one that addresses the ethical, mental, and physical aspects of winning a gunfight.

The author, Tim Rupp, has "been there" and "done that." Tim has real-world experience, which he applies in a powerful and masterful manner to guide the reader through the critical and essential process of getting your body, soul, and spirit prepared for the fight.

And we never needed this book more than we do now.

In the wake of the 9/11 terrorist attacks, Americans are rising to the challenge. Many states established shall-issue conceal-carry laws. Millions of Americans are buying and carrying guns. And if you believe (as I do) that every trained, armed citizen makes America a safer place, then you must believe in this book. Let me say that again: American is a safer place when we have trained, armed citizens. It is not enough to just buy and carry the gun. Now you must dedicate yourself—body, soul and spirit—to *Winning a Gunfight!*

Consider:

- What is the single, most horrendous international terrorist act in history? What is the single greatest body count, in a single incident, ever achieved by any non-governmental agency not in time of war? The World Trade Center on September 11, 2001...

- What is the single, most heinous domestic terrorist act in American history? What is the single greatest body count ever achieved in a terrorist act on American soil by an American Citizen? Oklahoma City...

- What is the highest body count of any criminal act on a college campus? Virginia Tech...

- What is the single greatest body count ever achieved by juvenile mass murderers in American history? Columbine High School...

- What is the single worst firearms massacre committed by a single individual in American history? The Pulse night club in Orlando, Florida.

...This is not some ancient history...not some distant land. This is us. Now.

There is a new twist to terrorism: It's called body count. Whether the perpetrators are school killers, workplace killers, or international terrorists, they are not interested in negotiating; their only goal is to kill as many people as humanly possible.

Shaken awake by the horror of these events, our citizens and our warriors will no longer sit by as innocent men, women, and children die in helpless mobs. We saw this new thinking on Sept 11, 2001, when Americans on the fourth airplane, Flight 93 over Pennsylvania, fought back. Americans have determined that they will not be victims!

This is America. Faced with a challenge like this, we don't take away rights. We give our citizens more rights! In many ways the most important right, the right that protects all the others, is the right to arm and protect ourselves and our loved ones. And, along with that right (as with any right) comes responsibility. The responsibility to train and prepare for that fateful day.

It will be extremely difficult for a terrorist to hijack another airplane and fly it into a building. Not just because of all the new security measures, but primarily because any idiot with a box cutter, or any fool who tries to set his shoe on fire, is going to have a planeload of passengers hopping up and down on his body. And if they DO succeed in hijacking a plane, it will immediately be shot out of the sky by the US Air Force.

No, they will probably not be able to use another plane as a weapon of mass destruction, but what they can do to us is what they have been doing in the Middle East for decades: active shooter strikes. In the Luxor massacre, at the Luxor, Egypt tourist site, a handful of armed Islamic extremists gunned down 62 tourists. The result was that they shut down the tourism business in Egypt for a year, costing that nation billions of dollars. THIS is the power of the terrorist, be they international or domestic: the ability to shut down a nation with just one strike.

The only viable response to a threat like this is to legally empower, physically arm, and properly train our citizens. We have been here before. Take the case of Massachusetts. In 1636 a frustrated General Court of the Massachusetts Bay Colony unanimously passed an ordinance that said:

> Whereas many complaints have been made to this Court, of the greatest neglect of all sorts of people of using the lawful and necessary means for their safety, especially in this time of so great danger from Indians, it is therefore ordered that no person shall travel above one mile from his dwelling without arms; upon pain of twelvepence for every default.

As pointed out by legendary author and firearms trainer, John Farnum, being unarmed was considered negligent. Self-protection was not just a personal responsibility; it was a duty to the community! And for over a century after the danger from hostile indigenous peoples was eliminated, there was no suggestion that this ordinance be repealed. A century and a half later, those people were the leaders of the armed rebellion that created the United States.

Today Massachusetts has strayed far from its roots. But, as J.R.R. Tolkien put it in *The Lord of the Rings*,

> Not all that is gold doth glitter,
> Not all those who wander are lost.
> The old that is strong does not whither,
> and the deep roots are not touched by the frost.

Now, in this dark hour, let us tap the strength that is drawn from those deep roots that have endured the bitter frost. Let us seek out the old that is strong and does not whither—the old ways, the ways of the pioneer and the gunslinger, in order to answer the challenge of the age.

And our forefathers also knew that it was not enough to just have a gun, it was also vital to be trained in the proper use of that weapon. In 1349, King Edward III of England told the citizens of London that their "skill of shooting" was being neglected, and he proclaimed that:

> [E]very one of the said city, strong in body, at leisure times on holidays, use in their recreation bow and arrows, or pellets or bolts, and learn and exercise the art of shooting...that they do not, after any manner apply themselves to the throwing of...handball, football, cambuck, or cockfighting, nor suchlike vain plays which have nor profit in them.

Teddy Roosevelt, while serving as President, said that:

We should establish shooting galleries in all the large public and military schools, should maintain national target ranges in different parts of the country, and should in every way encourage the formation of [shooting] clubs throughout all parts of the land.... It is unfortunately true that the great body of our citizens shoot less and less as time goes on. To meet this [challenge] we should encourage...practice...by every means in our power. Thus, and not otherwise, may we be able to assist in preserving the peace of the world. Fit to hold our own against the strong nations of the earth, our voice for peace will carry to the ends of the earth. Unprepared and therefore unfit, we must sit dumb and helpless to defend ourselves, protect others, or preserve peace. The first step— ...to avert war if possible, and to be fit for war if it should come—is to teach our men to shoot.

It bears repeating: our ancestors knew that it is not enough to just have a gun, it is also vital to be trained in the proper use of that weapon.

And that is what this book is all about. Here, in your hands, is one of the finest gunfighter training resources available. A veteran law enforcement officer and firearms trainer, a veteran of a real-world gunfight, with a career that spans four decades, Tim Rupp has applied his experiences and his expertise to guide the reader down the warrior path: body, soul and spirit. I strongly recommend that you read, study, and apply this excellent book.

Dave Grossman
Lt. Colonel, US Army (ret.)
Director, Killology Research Group, www.killology.com

"If possible, so far as it depends on you, live peaceably with all." (Romans 12:18)

More than Surviving

Chapter 1

Justified. Now what?

It was over. Nathaniel Williams lay on the ground suffering from three gunshot wounds that I inflicted. No one else was shot. Although he tried, Williams never got a shot off. The other two officers and I escaped unharmed. First aid was administered, emergency medical services (EMS) was summoned and transported the wounded assailant to the hospital. Patrol officers, police supervisors, crime scene detectives, and the Officer-Involved-Shooting Team from the San Antonio Police Department's (SAPD) homicide office converged on the scene to assist, collect evidence, and investigate. Between the numerous police officers, medical personal, detectives, and the news media, nearly 30 years later I still distinctly recall one person who showed up: Officer (now sergeant) Dave Evans. Dave, a good friend of mine, arrived shortly following the gunfight; he asked if I was alright. I assured him I was. Dave was not concerned about my physical welfare (he could see I sustained no physical injury); he was concerned about my mental and spiritual well-being. I had survived physically, but what about mentally and spiritually?

After being briefly questioned at the scene, I went to the homicide office. There I was afforded the opportunity to call a lawyer, was interviewed by detectives, wrote a report, and was relieved of my service revolver and ammunition. The handgun, spent casings, and live ammunition were taken to be processed as evidence. My sergeant issued me a temporary revolver and replacement ammunition on the spot. As per standard operating procedure I was placed on desk duty until the investigation was complete. The initial investigation by homicide took a couple months. After being cleared by the police department I was released from desk duty and allowed to return to my patrol shift and resume patrol duties. The homicide office forwarded their findings to the District Attorney's Office. Weeks later I was summoned to testify before a grand jury where once again I recalled the incident; and again it was determined that I acted within the law. The grand jury agreed my use of deadly force was justified.

The Three Parts of Humanity

Many people survive gunfights. In fact, most people who are in a gunfight survive. But there's a difference between surviving and winning. Surviving means you continue to exist. Continuing to exist and winning are not the same. Winning is more than "continuing to exist." Losers survive gunfights—winners secure victories. Winning means more than walking away. Winning means conquering. Winning means "success." Winning means "to gain." Winning means coming out better than when you went in. Even those who sustain serious physical injury can win a gunfight.

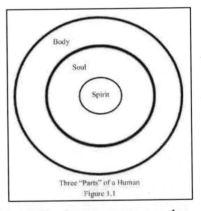

Three "Parts" of a Human
Figure 1.1

2

The purpose of this book is to teach you how to win a gunfight—not merely how to survive it. Firearms and tactical instructors can teach you how to physically survive a gunfight. As important

> *Losers survive gunfights—winners secure victories.*

as that is, there is more to a human being than a physical body. Proper tactics are designed to preserve the body, but there's also an ethical and mental part to every person. Some theologians tell us that we are made up of three parts: a body, a soul, and a spirit[3] (see figure 1.1). A common biblical text to support this position comes from the pen of the Apostle Paul who wrote, *"Now may the God of peace himself sanctify you completely, and may your whole **spirit** and **soul** and **body** be kept blameless at the coming of our Lord Jesus Christ"* (1 Thessalonians 5:23).[4]

Whether you believe the Bible or not, all of us probably recognize that there is more to who we are than a mere body. There is a physical, a mental, and an ethical aspect to each one of us. The soul/spirit are essential aspects that complete the whole. In a gunfight all three are involved. In fact, all three are involved in everything we do. It's important to keep in mind that each one of the three aspects (body, soul, and spirit) impacts the other two. Our spirit gives us a sense

| Spirit ⟶ Soul ⟶ Body |

of right and wrong; it's our ethical part. Our soul gives us our mental capacities; it's our intellect and where we make decisions about which specific actions to take. With the body we take action based on the decision made. You can imagine

---

[3] (Strauss, 2004)

[4] (Other biblical scholars say humans consist of two parts: a body and a soul/spirit. They understand Scripture to use the words translated as *soul* and *spirit* interchangeably. See Grudem, 1994, p. 472)

these three working together through this simple picture: a situation requiring a decision is facing you; your spirit quickly filters through the possible options and chooses the one that agrees with your ethics; your soul takes that choice and uses information gained through experience or training to formulate a plan of action; your body takes that plan of action and implements it to finalize your decision. I want to teach you how to train and prepare each of these three "parts", so that your whole can win a gunfight.

Body—The Importance of Being Tactically Sound

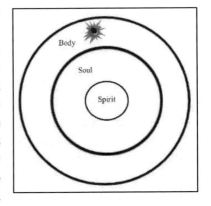

The human body is incredibly complex and re-silient. A very small minor-ity of people believe hu-mans consist only of a physical body. A more popular belief is that we are a higher animal form. This view is based on the theory that humans evolved into reasoning, rational, and moral beings. Another understanding is that God created hu-manity, either from nothing or through the use of an evolu-tionary process. No matter which of these viewpoints a per-son holds to, that fact is the human body is extremely com-plex and durable.

Medical science has taught us a great deal about our body. We understand that it is made up of several intercon-nected systems (e.g. respiratory, cardiovascular, and nerv-ous) that are critical for the body to survive. A gunshot wound is capable of disrupting these systems rendering the body incapable of survival. Military and police firearms and tactics instructors are charged with the ominous task of keep-ing their students alive in a gunfight.

Any professional firearms or tactics instructor will tell you how important proper training and preparation are *before* a gunfight. In the early days of professional policing, firearms training consisted primarily of marksmanship shooting. What is known today as tactical training and combat shooting for police was rare. Beginning in the 1970s firearms training started to transition from teaching basic marksmanship shooting skills to teaching shooting skills that are more practical for policing. Tactical training and combat shooting are designed to better prepare law enforcement officers for the kind of real-life shooting situations they will likely face in the course of their day-to-day duties. To tactically win a gunfight, you need to properly prepare for realistic shooting situations you will face when armed with a handgun.

Soul—The Importance of Being Mentally Sound

Although connected, the soul is distinct from the body. The body can be seen and touched. The soul cannot be seen nor can it be touched. The body is physical; the soul is an immaterial essence. The soul enables us to be in relationship to others. It is the "real" you. It is your per-

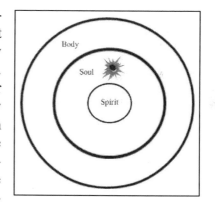

sonality, and the seat of your emotions (e.g. love—hate, courage—fear, joy—anger, happy—sad). In addition to our emotions, the soul is also where we do our thinking. We think, reason, contemplate, and ponder with our souls. With our souls we make decisions (do this—don't do that; go here—don't go there; yes—no, etc.).

According to the Farlex Medical Dictionary a person is considered clinically dead when there is "no pulse, no respiratory movement and no corneal reflex."[5] All of these are measurements of physical functions. Like an engine that stops when it runs out of fuel, a body–dies when its heart stops beating. But, is death really that simple? Is death merely the ceasing of physical functions?

The soul is critical to the body, because without it we are just a shell. The soul is the life in the physical body, and according to the Bible death actually occurs when the soul leaves the body.[6] Recently a friend's wife suffered a serious medical emergency and stopped breathing. She was transported to the hospital by ambulance and was kept alive by an artificial respirator that kept her circulatory and respiratory systems functioning. After some days the doctors informed him his wife would not recover. My friend told me he knew his wife had died long before her body was removed from the machines that were "keeping her alive."

So which is it? Is it "When the body ceases to function the soul departs?" or is it "When the soul departs the body ceases to function?" While the debate goes on between medical science and theology, we clearly understand that there is an essential link between the body and the soul. When these two parts are separated, in whichever order, death is imminent.

Now, a bullet can hit our bodies and not necessarily separate us from our souls—meaning we can be shot but physically survive. And since a bullet cannot hit our immaterial souls you might mistakenly assume that if it does not cause death, then it will not cause our soul any harm at all. However, the link between body and soul is so critical that separation is not the only factor to concern us. Remember, winning involves all three parts of our whole. The physical

---

[5] (Farlex Partner Medical Dictionary, 2012)
[6] (Genesis 35:18)

is often the most obvious—we must survive physically. But if we walk away from a gunfight without our mental health intact we haven't won. We must recognize that while a bullet can only physically harm the body, a gunfight can significantly affect the soul. In fact, a bullet doesn't even need to touch our body for a gunfight to touch our soul. This is what's known as *post-traumatic stress disorder* (PTSD).

> Post-traumatic stress disorder (PTSD) is a mental health condition that's triggered by a terrifying event—either experiencing it or witnessing it. Symptoms may include flashbacks, nightmares and severe anxiety, as well as uncontrollable thoughts about the event.[7]

Physical health relates to the body, mental health to the soul. The good news is that most people who experience a traumatic event will not get PTSD. The Mayo Clinic says, "Many people who go through traumatic events have difficulty adjusting and coping for a while, but they don't have PTSD—with time and good self-care, they usually get better."[8] The body recovers from a bullet wound with *time* and *good medical-care*. The soul recovers from a gunfight with *time* and *good self-care*. The tactical part of this book aims to teach you how to physically win a gunfight by out shooting an opponent. The mental part aims

> The body recovers from a bullet wound with *time* and *good medical-care*. The soul recovers from a gunfight with *time* and *good self-care*.

---

[7] (Mayo Clinic, 1998-2016)
[8] (Mayo Clinic, 1998-2016)

to teach you how to mentally win a gunfight by understanding what to expect, preparing in advance to make right decisions, and being aware of your surroundings.

Spirit—The Importance of Being Ethically Sound

There's more to you than a physical body and the mental capacity to reason, think, and relate to other people. Humans possess something animals do not—a "God awareness." The Judeo-Christian understanding is that human beings are made in the image and likeness of God; and

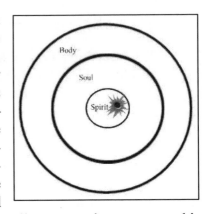

just as God's fingerprints are all over creation so too are his fingerprints on the heart of humanity.[9] We are different from animals—we are ethical creatures.

If you remember, one of the distinctions between soul and body is the soul's inability to be touched. Truly, it cannot be touched *physically*, but as discussed it can be touched *emotionally*. Why is that? Humans get stressed-out, have anxiety attacks, and suffer from PTSD because we are ethical creatures; and unlike animals, humans experience remorse, shame, and guilt. Guilt is "bearing responsibility for an offense or wrongdoing; [or the] remorseful awareness of having done something wrong."[10] Another definition is "Guilt is both a cognitive and an emotional experience that occurs when a person believes that he or she has violated a moral standard and is responsible for that violation."[11] If there's a wrong, then there must be a right. If there is a moral

---

[9] (Genesis 1:26; Ecclesiastes 3:11; Romans 1:19-20; 2:15)
[10] (Nelson's New Illustrated Bible Dictionary, 1995, p. 526)
[11] (Therapists.com, 2016)

standard, then someone must set that standard. Who says what's right or wrong? Who has that moral authority?

> *"He who thinks half-heartedly will not believe in God; but he who really thinks has to believe in God."*
> —Isaac Newton

A recent Gallup poll revealed that 92% of Americans believe in God.[12] That means 92% of Americans understand the ultimate authority is God, and recognize that his authority is supreme to humanity. So, when we violate a moral standard set in place by One in authority over us, we feel shame and remorse.

Humans' "God-awareness" causes us to do things animals do not. Animals don't worship. Animals react and respond instinctively. They protect themselves and their own without regard to law or rules of engagement. Animals kill other animals without regard to ethical implications. And they don't know right from wrong. Mankind is different. We worship, react and respond out of reason—or even against reason! We protect our own, but do so with regard to law and rules of engagement. We act with regard to *ethical* implications. We know right from wrong. Anthropologists confirm that throughout all cultures there is a moral code inside every person. John Stott writes "to everybody everywhere...there is a difference between right and wrong, and that evil deserves to be punished."[13]

If you are going to walk away from a gunfight as a winner then you need to know how to bring this final part of your whole self into that battle. Remaining alive means your body won. Remaining sane means your mind won. And finally, remaining justified means your spirit won. This means you must be convinced in your heart of the moral and ethical

---

[12] (Gallup, 2016)
[13] (Stott as quoted by Osborne, 2004, p. 48)

implications of using deadly force against another person before arming yourself with a lethal weapon. Even in cases of self-defense or defense of another innocent victim, not everyone is comfortable with using force that may take the life of another person.

Conclusion

It is critical to address all three parts: body, soul, and spirit. The spirit is where it all begins. When we learn and understand the ethical and moral standards of the Person to whom we must answer, only then do we have the information needed to make the "right" decision and to act on that decision. If we act without thinking, we get in trouble. If we decide without regard to the moral and ethical implications, we get in trouble. The best course of action is to prepare the spirit, soul, and body before we decide to arm ourselves with a lethal weapon.

Part One

The Spirit

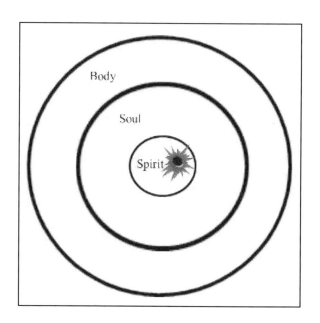

Dealing with Guilt

Chapter 2

The spirit is the ethical part. The spirit says, "It's right or it's wrong."

Guilt

Time and witnesses are critical in murder cases. A suspect is identified within 72 hours of most murder cases that are cleared by arrest. After three days with no suspect it becomes far less likely that any will ever be identified. The lack of eyewitnesses means detectives must hope the physical evidence will point to the identity of the murderer and connect him to the crime. Homicide detectives quickly learn that the "found" or "dumped" body cases are usually the hardest to solve. Why? Time and witnesses.

At the San Antonio Police Department, cases were assigned each morning at 7:30 at the Homicide Unit's roll call. On Thursday, April 8th, 1993, I was assigned a murder that had occurred overnight. It was a found body case; and of course there were no witnesses to the murder, and no suspects. A young couple walking through the area discovered the body of a Hispanic male behind an abandoned gas station and called the police. The Night Criminal Investigation Division detectives, the Crime Scene unit, and an investigator

13

from the Medical Examiner's Office responded and processed the crime scene. I reviewed the reports and the statements from the couple who discovered the body, but it didn't give me much to go on—not even the victim's name. I checked a car out from the carpool and headed to the morgue to observe the autopsy and speak with the medical examiner. I was hoping for more physical evidence. The doctor said the unidentified male was stabbed several times and beaten. Two stab wounds were near the heart, either of which would have been fatal. I photographed the body and jotted down my observations. Robbery? It was common for downtown drunks to be rolled for their money, but rarely were they killed. Another thing that didn't fit a stranger attack were the number of stab wounds. "Overkill" during the crime indicated anger or hate—a personal vengeance. It seemed the murderer(s) knew the victim. But that was just speculation on my part.

Later that day, I went to the crime scene to look around and attempt to locate any witnesses to the murder. I found a 42-year-old African-American man hanging around the area. He claimed to have seen four Hispanic males drinking at the location where the body was discovered the previous night. He didn't know their names, but said they frequented the downtown area. In more than a decade of policing I'd learned a few things about street people—one of which was their hesitancy to cooperate with the police. My newly found witness seemed overzealous to provide me with sketchy and inconsistent information; but I needed to follow-up on it, if for no other reason than it was all I had. After wasting a full day running around, I was unable to substantiate any of the leads provided by my "witness". I was at a dead end.

The next day the Medical Examiner's Office identified the victim as Mr. Gregorio Garcia;[14] but his next of kin and current address couldn't be found. No one called the police to report him missing or to ask about him. Time went on with no leads. Finally, more than ten days after the murder, Mr. Garcia's sister, Ida, showed up at the Homicide Office to inquire about the case and said she had information about her brother's girlfriend. Ida said Mr. Garcia's girlfriend was a lady named Elvira who frequented Bertha's Bar on San Antonio's Westside.

Over the next several days I was able to identify and then locate Elvira. She didn't have a permanent residence and spent most of her waking hours in bars, splitting time living with one of her two daughters after the bars closed. It was clear Elvira was living a destructive lifestyle and her children were worried. As I was able to peel back the layers of relationships, and decipher between truth and lies, I found that Raul, Elvira's 27-year-old son, blamed Mr. Garcia for his mother's lifestyle. All of Elvira's family lived on the city's Westside, miles from the murder scene except two—a daughter and a granddaughter, both of whom lived in public housing projects about half a mile from the murder scene. The daughter was uncooperative and denied any knowledge about the murder. However, the granddaughter, Sylvia, said her uncle, Raul, and a cousin, James, showed up at her house the night of the murder. She said Raul and James entered her house sometime after midnight and went straight to a backroom without saying a word. Suspicious, Sylvia checked on them and discovered they both had blood on their clothes. Raul was in the bathroom washing off a knife. The duo confessed to Sylvia they had attacked Mr. Garcia by beating and stabbing him. Finally, there was a break in the case.

---

[14] The names in this case have been changed to protect the privacy of those involved.

For the next week I attempted to contact an elusive James. James was several years younger than Raul and I believed he was the weak link. Sylvia said Raul was the instigator and James went along at Raul's bidding. But James remained evasive and refused to respond to any of my messages. A family that was less than enthusiastic to cooperate didn't help. On April 30th, 22 days after Mr. Garcia's body was discovered, I learned James had left town to stay with his father in New Braunfels, Texas. I turned my attention to Raul. I located him that afternoon. Raul had been bouncing all over the Westside staying with friends. To my surprise, the nervous suspect was more than willing to come in for an interview. But not to my surprise, he denied any knowledge of the murder and claimed he was miles from the crime scene on the fateful night.

After three weeks the case came to a screeching halt. I had two suspects, Raul and James, but no evidence to tie either one to the crime. Sylvia, the only witness, was a relative that didn't actually witness the murder and refused to provide a written statement. Sylvia's verbal statement about Raul and James having blood on their clothes, the knife, their admission to her, and two nervous suspects was all I had. I knew the District Attorney wouldn't even look at the case with no physical evidence to confirm Sylvia's story. Besides, Sylvia's story was likely to change before it went to court since she refused to give a written statement.

The following week I was in the office catching up on paperwork, reviewing cases, and writing reports. It was one of those days I was happy I made detective—the rain was coming down in buckets outside. It had been raining all morning and into the afternoon when my phone rang. The secretary said there was someone at the front desk who wanted to speak with me. At the reception area I found a soaking wet Raul with his head hung in shame.

We went to my desk and Raul confessed to the murder. I typed out his confession and he signed it. Raul, who didn't have a car, who had to take busses from the far Westside where he lived all the way downtown, was confessing to murder. "Why?" I asked him. "Guilt" was his response. He couldn't live with the fact that he murdered a man and needed to confess to his crime.

A Universal Human Condition

Guilt is a universal human condition. In chapter one guilt was defined as "bearing responsibility for an offense or wrongdoing; [or the] remorseful awareness of having done something wrong"[15] and as "a cognitive and an emotional experience that occurs when a person believes that he or she has violated a moral standard and is responsible for that violation."[16] One psychologist believes that "a sense of guilt occurs when we violate our own inner code of conduct. Guilt is a message of disapproval from the conscience which says, in effect, 'You should be ashamed of yourself!'"[17] Without exception, everyone is guilty of violating acceptable standards of behavior. The standards we break may be family codes, school rules, work policies, or even criminal laws. Breaking the rules is called an *offense*. An offense is "something that is wrong or improper; something that causes a person to be hurt, angry or upset."[18]

When we break an ethical standard and hurt someone the relationship with that person is harmed and we experience guilt. According to an article on the *Psychology Today* website, "It's appropriate to feel guilty when you've done something wrong. Feeling the emotion of guilt for an action deserving of remorse is normal; to not feel guilty, in these

---

[15] (Nelson's New Illustrated Bible Dictionary, 1995, p. 526)
[16] (Therapists.com, 2016)
[17] (Dobson, 2016)
[18] (Merriam-Webster, 2016)

cases, may be a sign of psychopathy."[19] A psychopathic personality creates someone who is entirely self-absorbed. They have no regard for anyone other than themselves. Their lack of both a conscience and a moral responsibility to others becomes evident through antisocial behavior. This is an abnormal response to an offense.

Rather, it's normal to seek forgiveness and work to restore the relationship. By making amends for our actions we seek to ease our guilt. But why is this the normal behavior and not the abnormal one? Why do we feel guilty? We do so because we have a conscience, a moral compass, and we desire to maintain healthy relationships with others. For Raul, his conscience could only be eased by confessing to the murder he committed. Guilt is a healthy emotion when it drives us to do the right thing.

But there's also an unhealthy guilt. This occurs when we are eaten up by shame or blameworthiness for harm done to another over which we are not responsible. This feeling is called *false guilt* because it manifests many of the same feelings as healthy guilt, but the feelings are not derived from a true offense. They come from a lie that says we bear personal responsibility as an offender for: something we didn't do (e.g. we weren't there to stop the harm); something we unintentionally did (e.g. we harmed someone by accident); something we were justified in doing (e.g. we shot someone who we believed was a threat). In America today, there is an aversion to harming anyone for any reason. This has led to police officers (and others who come to the aid of innocent victims) suffering from false guilt.

False guilt can be brought on by a variety of situations. It's not uncommon for people to attempt "suicide by cop" in order to take their own life. "Suicide by cop" is intentionally presenting a deadly threat to a police officer to entice the officer to shoot. Another situation that brings false

---

[19] (Whitbourne, 2012)

guilt to police officers is using deadly force against innocent persons. Officers are trained to respond to a posed threat of any kind. When the stakes are high unfortunate events can occur. For instance, our enemies in both combat and the war on terror understand our aversion to harming innocent people; hence, they use civilians as human shields, or to carry out bombings. Also, there are people who misrepresent themselves to police using toy or nonlethal guns. This puts police officers in precarious situations. Shooting an innocent person that appears to be a valid threat to the officer, fellow officers, or other innocents can lead to false guilt.

The taking of human life is a serious matter. It seems to go against everything we've been taught from our Judeo-Christian values. Human life is different from all other forms of life. Taking the life of another human being is different from killing an animal. The Bible says that humanity was made in the image of God.[20]

In righteous judgment God destroyed human life in the great Flood. In his grace and mercy God saved Noah and his family through the great Flood. Following the Flood, God told Noah just how precious human life was. The value of something is determined by what it cost, Noah was told that a person who takes the life of another would have to pay with his own life. In Genesis chapter nine the Lord instituted human government and capital punishment, *"From his fellow man I will require a reckoning for the life of man. 'Whoever sheds the blood of man, by man shall his blood be shed, for God made man in his own image'"* (Gen. 9:5-6).

Yes, the taking of human life is a serious matter. Nevertheless there is a time when the protection of the innocent involves killing an aggressor. King Solomon, the wise king and man of peace recognized this fact; he wrote, *"For everything there is a season, and a time for every matter under heaven: a time to be born, and a time to die; a time to*

---

[20] (Genesis 1:27)

19

plant, and a time to pluck up what is planted; a time to kill..." (Ecc. 3:1-3).

But not everyone is willing to pull the trigger.

The willingness to pull the trigger

Dying can't be undone. The human body can withstand severe abuse and torture, physically, emotionally, and mentally. But once a person is dead, there's no coming back.[21] Having been taught the value of human life, it's no wonder there's such a reluctance to kill in our society—even in the face of a deadly threat. West Point psychology professor and former army ranger, Lt. Col. Dave Grossman has done extensive study about the reluctance of soldiers on the battlefield to kill. After the rifle replaced the longbow as the standard issue weapon for soldiers the kill rate in war should have skyrocketed, but as Grossman discovered,

> The weak link between the killing potential and the killing capability of these units [military units armed with rifles] was the soldier. The simple fact is that when faced with a living, breathing, opponent instead of a target, a significant majority of the soldiers revert to a posturing mode in which they fire over their enemy's heads.[22]

Bill Jordan comments on the reality of facing another human being trying to kill you,

> No normal man likes the thought of using a lethal weapon upon another human.... You

---

[21] This of course is in the natural order of things. God, who is above nature, can raise the dead back to life. Jesus is the prime example.
[22] (Grossman, On Killing, 1996, p. 11)

are struck with the realization that your opposition is a man who is trying to kill you and that in the next instant the world may have to find someone else to revolve about. His bullet may end life for you! Nothing in your prior experience, except gunfighting, can prepare you for this shocking thought.[23]

Kenneth Murray says this unwillingness to kill can be linked to police officers hesitating to pull the trigger in self-defense. Murray blames this on "societal preconditioning."[24] Although, if you watch what comes out of Hollywood you'd think Americans had no problem pulling the trigger. Murray notes, "Contrary to the relative ease with which TV lawmen dispatch the Tinseltown villains, killing another human being is not as simple as pointing a gun and pulling a trigger, although mechanically that's really all there is to it."[25] Humans, especially those raised in a Western Christian culture, are reluctant to take the life of another human being.

> *"No normal man likes the thought of using a lethal weapon upon another human."*
> —Bill Jordan

Mike Wood, in his tactical analysis of the Newhall shooting in which four California Highway Patrol troopers were gunned down, makes this observation,

The officers also had an additional challenge, because they were good men who were not immersed in a world of violence. They were raised in good families and were busy starting families of their own.... They fixed cars, attended barbeques, painted the baby's room,

---

[23] (Jordan, 1965, pp. 101, 105)
[24] (Murray K. R., 2004, p. 20)
[25] (Murray K. R., 2004, p. 19)

hugged their spouses, attended church, changed diapers, planned for the future, and did a million other everyday things completely unrelated to preparing for violent combat. They were raised in and lived in a culture that discouraged violence and stamped all kinds of hidden imprints on their brain that would cause hesitation to use force, even when it was justified and necessary.[26]

The simple fact is that without a willingness to kill the enemy our nation will not survive. Without the willingness of police officers to kill those wanting to kill us our society will not survive. From our American Revolution to our current war on terror and in the cities, towns, villages, and countrysides throughout our nation, America has always had those willing to face killers and kill them. According to Grossman, "The only thing that is holding our society together is the warrior....

> *"Were we to go one generation without warriors our society would cease to exist."*
> —Dave Grossman

Were we to go one generation without warriors our society would cease to exist."[27] Grossman defines a warrior as one who has the authority and capability to march toward the sound of the gun (face interpersonal human aggression) and return fire (operate under those conditions).[28]

The Bible has a lot to say about warriors and mighty men who fight and kill the enemy. First Chronicles 11:10-47 is a record of David's mighty men. The list includes: Jashobeam who *"wielded his spear against 300 whom he killed at one time."*; Eleazar who *"took his stand...and killed the Philistines."*; and Abishai (David's nephew) who

---

[26] (Wood, 2013, p. 133)
[27] (Grossman, The Bullet Proof Mind audio seminar, 1995)
[28] (Grossman, The Bullet Proof Mind audio seminar, 1995)

"wielded his spear against 300 men and killed them." Why does the Bible list these mighty men and give an account of how they killed so many in battle? Because they were warriors for Israel. They protected Israel against the enemy. These men weren't enshrined in the biblical record because they were killers, but because they were warriors who were willing to kill to protect the people of their nation. In America we have monuments to our warriors.

Where do warriors come from? Many people are unwilling to use deadly force against another human being, and that's okay. That's the way God has made them. We need these people. These are some of the finest humans on the planet. Perhaps King Solomon was one. The Bible shares an interesting story about King David and his son.

> *David said to Solomon, "My son, I had it in my heart to build a house to the name of the LORD my God. But the word of the LORD came to me, saying, 'You have shed much blood and have waged great wars. You shall not build a house to my name, because you have shed so much blood before me on the earth. Behold, a son shall be born to you who shall be a man of rest. I will give him rest from all his surrounding enemies. For his name shall be Solomon, and I will give peace and quiet to Israel in his days.* (1 Chr. 22:7-9)

While I believe there's an innate sense in all humans to protect their own family, I also believe instilled in the hearts of some is a warrior spirit—the spirit of a protector. However, even in warriors there remains an averseness to use deadly force against another human being, which may cause hesita-

tion. Whether this is a result of social conditioning or some other psychological factor, I don't know. The question is, "Can we tap into the warriors among us and give them the authority and capability to march toward the sound of gunfire and take action?"

Police Lt. James Como believes we can do this with a proper mindset and training by internalizing what he calls the "warrior spirit":

> If one is truly to become a warrior-protector, one must embrace the belief system and make it a life-style. It is inviting disaster if one believes that it is something that can be turned on and off at will. Only when one has truly internalized the warrior spirit can growth in the area of 'proactive' self-defense and tactical decision-making begin.[29]

---

[29] (Como as quoted by Murray, 2006, p. 20)

Grossman continues this same argument when he explains,

> [M]odern training or conditioning techniques can partially overcome the inclination to posture [not pull the trigger at the moment of truth]. Indeed, the history of warfare can be seen as a history of increasingly more effective mechanisms for enabling and conditioning men to overcome their innate resistance to killing their fellow human beings.[30]

However, prior to training the mind and body, the spirit needs to be at peace. Before strapping on a gun to protect yourself or another, you must ask yourself, "Are you willing to kill another human being?" If the answer is "No", that's okay, but you should not be carrying a firearm. The purpose of carrying a gun for protection isn't to threaten someone with the hope they will give up. What if they don't? Are you willing to pull the trigger?

> *"If one is truly to become a warrior-protector, one must embrace the belief system and make it a life-style."*
> —James Como

Let me be clear. In the event you must use lethal force the goal is to quickly neutralize (that is to stop) an armed aggressor before the aggressor is able to harm any innocent person. To *quickly neutralize* is key. Response to an armed aggressor must be immediate and effective. To neutralize a threat is to nullify it. While the goal is to end the threat, it may cost the aggressor his life. Those willing to carry a gun to defend life must be willing to take it.

Not long ago the King James Version (KJV) of the Bible was the most widely used Bible in North America. The

---

[30] (Grossman, On Killing, 1996, p. 13)

25

KJV's translation of the sixth commandment has caused undo stress for soldiers, police officers, and those defending themselves or others by using deadly force. The KJV translation reads, *"Thou shalt not kill"* (Exod. 20:13). *"Thou shalt not kill"* was often misunderstood as a divine and absolute prohibition against *any* taking of human life. However, as has already been demonstrated from Scripture, there is no absolute prohibition against the taking of human life.

Later English translations of the Bible are more accurate when they use the word *murder* rather than *kill*, i.e. *"You shall not murder."* Kill is to take the life of another; murder is to do so with malice, that is, with evil intent. The Bible tells us God looks at our intentions or heart, *"For the Lord sees not as man sees: man looks on the outward appearance, but the Lord looks on the heart"* (1 Sam. 16:7). Jesus affirms the same in the New Testament saying that murder is a matter of the heart.[31]

Murder is to kill another human being without justification. The Hebrew word (רָצַח) translated as *kill* or *murder* can mean either. Therefore in Hebrew, like in English, context dictates which definition is intended by the writer. Numbers 35:30 is an example of this same Hebrew word (רָצַח) translated *kill* in the sixth commandment having different meanings in the same verse. Here's the KJV's translation where the Hebrew word (רָצַח) is translated as *murderer* and *death* in the same verse: *"...the murderer shall be put to death...."* The New Living Translation renders it: *"All murderers must be put to death."* In this text Moses uses the same word but means different things, he is saying a murderer (one who kills another without justification) is to be put to death (killed by the government with justification).

As noted before, all killing certainly cannot be against God's law or he would never have sanctioned and even commanded the deaths of Israel's enemies throughout

---

[31] (Mark 7:20-23)

the Old Testament. And even in the New Testament Jesus himself never condemns the Roman soldiers for carrying out all their duties. The command not to kill refers to unjustified killing that is outside the law[32]—we call it murder. The command not to murder is an absolute prohibition against the *unauthorized* or *unjustified* taking of human life. You must understand that nowhere does the Bible prohibit the *lawful* use of deadly force to defend innocent life. It's the *unlawful* use of force that is prohibited in Scripture.

Conclusion

The spirit is the ethical part. The spirit says, "It's right or it's wrong." The spirit informs the soul (or mind) of what the principled implications are to a decision. Guilt is brought on when we violate a moral or ethical value. As shown, there is no moral or ethical prohibition against using deadly force by either the God of the Bible or Western civilization's laws and values. However, you must understand that there are some in society who believe it is wrong to take human life in any circumstance. That's okay, because America is a free country where people are free to believe as they wish. What you must believe and understand is that neither the Bible, nor America's laws support that position. So, the question to you becomes, "If necessary, are you willing to use force that will likely cause seriously bodily injury, or even death, to another human being?" Simply put, "Are you willing to pull the trigger?" Even after knowing and acknowledging that there is no prohibition to use deadly force, you must be willing to pull the trigger. After, and only after, the spiritual or ethical issue is addressed and put to rest can training begin.

---

[32] (Stuart, 2006, p. 462)

Part Two

The Soul

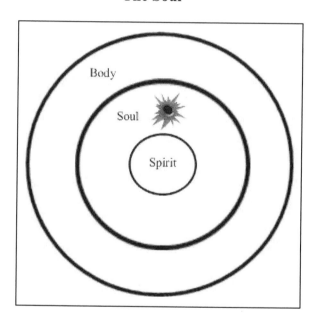

Make a Decision!

Chapter 3

The soul is the mental part. The mind says, "Do this; don't do that."

Expect the Unexpected

In 2004, a veteran law enforcement officer in Western Montana experienced the unexpected when a suspect drew a pistol on him. However, it wasn't the pistol draw that created the tension, which led to a mentally unprepared officer being placed in danger and endanger the lives of others. What was it?

As a SWAT officer, firearms trainer, use-of-force instructor, superb shot, and veteran of deadly force encounters this man had all the credentials to hold him in good stead. So when he heard the call over his police radio that shots were fired at officers in a small town just to the east and the suspect was now speeding towards him along Montana state highway 200, he didn't hesitate to put himself in position to stop the assailant. He planned to force the vehicle into a shallow reservoir and end the threat. Unfortunately, the suspect was able to maneuver past the officer and continue speeding down the road. The vehicle stopped at a 24-hour convenience store just down the road. When the deputy pulled in, the suspect was waiting—gun in hand.

31

Suddenly, the seasoned police veteran was face-to-face with not only a gun pointed at him, but at a cute, petite, young blonde holding the weapon. He had daughters her age! And just like that, he found himself mentally unprepared to respond. Facing a gunman wasn't something he had just trained and prepared for, but something he had experienced. But a gun*woman*—that was different. He reluctantly drew his service pistol as he exited his vehicle, and began entreating the woman to lower her weapon. The deputy continued to struggle with his internal assessment of the threat she posed. Even as she wavered between pointing the gun at him and herself, the officer could not reconcile her actions with the way young ladies are "supposed" to act.

The deputy, like many other officers, joined the ranks of law enforcement to protect women and children, not to shoot them. This made his interaction with the girl all the more complicated. On one hand, she resembled those he swore to protect, but on the other hand, she was pointing a gun at him. Clearly flustered that the deputy wouldn't shoot her, the victim took advantage of the officer's hesitation to act due to his unprepared and conflicted mental state. She ran to a nearby ball field and shot herself in the chest, but not fatally. She was treated for her wounds and later booked into jail.

Years later, I interviewed the deputy, and he told me that his fundamental morals and values made it difficult for him to even draw his weapon, much less point it at the woman who threated to shoot him. She didn't fit the profile of the "dirt bags" he was trained to confront and with whom he'd become accustomed to dealing.

However, he chose to use the encounter as a learning experience for himself and his agency. He modified his agency's firearms training by incorporating more realistic targets. Rather than simply shooting nondescript gray silhouettes, he began using life-size cardboard silhouette targets "dressed" in women's clothing. What he found astounded him. Just as he hesitated shooting in a real-life situation, he saw his fellow officers hesitate during these new training scenarios. The deputy realized there needed to be specific instruction on mentally preparing to face a threat that did not fit a preconceived notion of an assailant. Through repetition in practice and training, the officers began to accept that anyone with a firearm is capable of posing a threat. These newly trained officers were now prepared mentally to quickly and accurately assess a situation regardless of an assailant's profile.

Colonel Jeff Cooper, one of the foremost authorities on defense weapons, understands the importance of being mentally in the game. Colonel Cooper, in his classic handbook, *The Principles of Personal Defense*, explains in simple terms,

> [M]any men who are not cowards are simply unprepared for the fact of human savagery. They have not thought about it...and they just don't know what to do. When they look right into the face of depravity or violence, they are astonished and confounded. This can be corrected.[33]

To correct this unpreparedness, the mind needs to be conditioned to respond properly to a threat. In recent years, photographic targets depicting real adults of both genders wearing a wide variety of clothing have become common in police, military, and security training. However, I have yet to see juveniles portrayed. It seems that even with

> *"Many men who are not cowards are simply unprepared for the fact of human savagery."*
> —Jeff Cooper

[33] (Cooper, 1972, p. 17)

the proliferation of young assassins in school shootings we are still averse to the idea of training to shoot children.

Flight or Fight...or Fright?

For years psychologists have taught us that there are two responses to fear: flight or fight. I remember being taught that when faced with danger and fear kicks in we will either run from danger (flight) or confront danger (fight). Lt. Col. Grossman disagrees that there are but two responses to fear. Grossman says there are at least two additional responses to fear when the threat comes from another human: posturing and submitting.[34]

According to Grossman, soldiers have historically postured by wearing uniforms or armament that made them look larger, displaying weaponry that made them appear stronger, and shooting blasts from muskets and cannons over the enemies' heads intimidating them into surrender.[35] However, when it becomes necessary to draw a pistol and engage an assailant, the time for posturing has passed. For example, when an assailant appears with a gun in a room full of people, posturing is not a valid response. Further, posturing against those with the mindset that they have come to kill until they are killed will not be an effective tool. Posturing will only work on those who are themselves afraid of being defeated or dying.

Posturing is an attempt to appear stronger, bigger, or in some way superior to one's enemy. When I was in high school my buddy's truck broke down and I decided to borrow some tools, so I headed for a nearby house. Half way across the front yard a large German shepherd lurched from the front porch and bounded toward all 135 pounds of a scrawny 16-year-old boy—me. Wide-eyed and scared my

---

[34] (Grossman, On Killing, 1996, p. 5)
[35] (Grossman, On Killing, 1996, pp. 5-16)

first thought was to run, but I knew I'd never outrun the beast. I also knew I'd be no match in a one-on-one fight. Having a dog of my own, I was hoping this German shepherd would respond to a threatening command. I decided to posture (although I didn't know the technical name for it at the time) by threatening him. Turning to face the charging monster that was now only a few feet from his prey, I looked into the eyes of my foe and yelled with the loudest command voice I could muster, "NO!" The dog stopped in its tracks. I pointed back to the porch and issued a second command, "Get back over there!" To my surprise, and great relief, the now timid canine obeyed while I turned and quickly made it back to the safety of the truck.

The second response Grossman adds to the flight-or-fight response is submission. I call this the "fright" response. Fright is the "dumb-and-numb" response. This response is caused by sensory overload. The heart rate is upwards of 175 beats per minute, there's a loss of fine motor skills, and vision and hearing are adversely affected. Grossman calls this "Condition Black," and explains, "As you enter Condition Black, your cognitive processing deteriorates, which is a fancy way of saying you stop thinking."[36] Condition Black and other conditions are discussed in chapter six.

The first three responses (flight, fight, and posture) are responses to a threat with the goal of removing the threat. The flight response seeks to remove the danger by creating distance between you and the opponent. The fight response seeks to overpower an opponent and win the battle. The posturing response seeks to intimidate the attacker making him believe he cannot prevail. All three of these responses come out of rational thinking. You've heard the expressions "scared stiff," "stage fright," or "paralyzed with fear." The fright response comes out of not thinking. When you can't think you can't act, therefore you submit.

---

[36] (Grossman, On Combat, 2008, pp. 31-44)

In Roseburg, Oregon, on October 2, 2015 students were in classes at Umpqua Community College when confronted by an armed assailant. Media reports demonstrated that many of the victims were in a state of fright, taking no action to save their own lives. The students took no action, even as the assailant paused to reload and ask questions. They simply submitted to the gunman's demands.

> The gunman who opened fire at Oregon's Umpqua Community College targeted Christians specifically, according to the father of a wounded student. Before going into spinal surgery, Anastasia Boylan told her father and brother the gunman entered her classroom firing. The professor in the classroom was shot point blank. Others were hit, she told her family.
>
> Everyone in the classroom dropped to the ground.
>
> The gunman, while reloading his handgun, ordered the students to stand up if they were Christians, Boylan told her family.
>
> "And they would stand up and he said, 'Good, because you're a Christian, you're going to see God in just about one second,'" Boylan's father, Stacy, told CNN, relaying her account.
>
> "And then he shot and killed them."[37]

---

[37] (Cable News Network, 2015)

However, one student refused to be a victim and took action—30 year-old Chris Mintz refused to submit. Rather than doing what the gunman ordered, he charged the gunman and was shot seven times for his bravery. Mr. Mintz, an army veteran, survived the shooting and is credited with saving the lives of other students.[38] What was the difference between Mr. Mintz and those who were "dumb and numb"? The difference was conditioning. Because he never entered into Condition Black he was able to think. He understood the assailant wasn't going to quit the killing unless stopped. It was likely his army training that helped Mr. Mintz "keep his cool", think, and respond to the threat.

As school children we were conditioned to respond to the sound of a fire alarm. We stopped what we were doing, formed a line, and exited the building while calmly following behind each other as teachers ensured everyone was out. We didn't need to think—we just responded. We responded because we were conditioned to respond to a particular stimulus in a predetermined way. When fire alarms blared throughout the school it startled us, but we quickly identified the sound and responded as conditioned. We had heard the sound before. We had made plans. We responded as planned.

Imagine if there were no fire drills, teachers had never planned, and students were never trained. What do you think the response would be in the event of a real fire? There would be mass chaos. Many school children would simply shut down, submitting to the dangers of a fire, and burn to death. Over the years countless lives were saved from fire because teachers and students were conditioned to respond to a particular stimulus in a predetermined way.

In an interview shortly after the San Bernardino massacre, Detroit police Chief James Craig, said this about armed and trained citizens,

---

[38] (USA Today Network and KGW Staff, 2015)

The reality of the world that I work in and have now for 38 years, is that we respond and react to situations. And if an emergency call for service comes in, shots fired, a massive shooting, terrorist act, we're responding. So in those seconds, those brief seconds, when the first shots are fired, it might be that armed citizen...that law-abiding citizen that's trained.[39]

Conclusion

Just like it's important to respond automatically to a fire alarm, the best chance of winning a gunfight is to respond automatically. That makes preparation and training a necessity. There are fundamentals that must be learned in order to have a proper response to a deadly assault on you or one you are protecting. Fright is not a proper response, but the only way to avoid being "dumb-and-numb" is through a conditioned response. Preparation and training are required to elicit the only acceptable responses of flight or fight. Again, conditioned responses are achieved only through proper preparation and training.

---

[39] (Live interview with Neil Cavuto, *Your World with Neil Cavuto*, December 4, 2015)

Training—for Reality

Chapter 4

The Newhall Shooting

Police learned the hard way that responding during a gunfight is a direct result of training and preparation. In the spring of 1970, two ex-convicts, Jack Twining and Bobby Davis, were traveling through southern California intent on engaging in their own mini crime wave. The ex-cons met and befriended one another in prison; both were released less than a year earlier. The duo planned to rob an armored truck delivering cash to the Santa Anita Racetrack. To pull off the robbery, they planned to steal dynamite from a construction site near the city of Newhall, and on the night of April 5, 1970, the felons began to execute their plan. Davis drove their red Pontiac coupe northbound on the Golden State Highway. North of Newhall, they pulled onto the shoulder and stopped near the construction site. Davis waited in the car while Twining went in search of the explosives.

Sitting alone in the Pontiac, Davis became nervous about appearing conspicuous, so he made a quick U-turn, but while crossing the median to the southbound lane he nearly hit another car. The car stopped and the couple inside jotted down the Pontiac's license plate number and then pulled up alongside the Pontiac to confront Davis. When they approached Davis he pointed a .38 caliber revolver at the driver. The frightened couple sped off and called the police to report the incident.

A short time later, California Highway Patrol (CHP) troopers Roger Gore and Walt Frago spotted the Pontiac traveling southbound. Exiting at Newhall, the red coupe pulled into a parking lot shared by J's Restaurant and a Standard gas station. It was here that the troopers planned to contact the suspect.

There was only supposed to be one suspect, but when

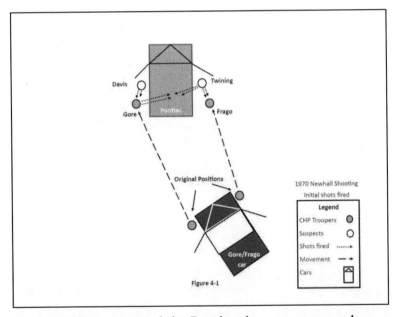

Figure 4-1

Gore and Frago stopped the Pontiac they saw a second man in the passenger seat. Davis stopped the car before pulling all the way into the parking lot, forcing Gore to stop the CHP cruiser at an angle about 20 feet behind the suspects' vehicle. The cruiser's angle provided cover for Gore behind the front left fender, but left the passenger side of the car exposed to the suspects' vehicle (see figure 4-1). Frago exited the passenger side of the patrol car, shotgun held at port-arms (the shotgun held in front of the body with muzzle pointed up and to the left, not towards the threat). Frago had not chambered a round in the shotgun. At that time, CHP had a policy requiring a tape seal over the forend on a shotgun. Chambering a round would break the seal, and any trooper breaking a seal was required to provide a written report to the patrol sergeant detailing why a round was chambered. The intent of this policy was to discourage officers from using their shotguns. It was an effective policy.

It was 11:54 pm when Gore and Frago stopped the Pontiac. From a position behind the left fender, Gore drew his revolver and pointed it at the suspects while he ordered them to exit the car. Davis finally complied after a number of commands and stepped from the driver's seat and stood next to the Pontiac. Ignoring the orders, Twining remained in the passenger seat. Both officers approached the suspect vehicle. While holding Davis at gunpoint, Gore ordered him to spread his legs and place his hands on top of the car. Davis followed his instructions.

While Gore was dealing with Davis, Frago focused his attention on Twining and approached the passenger's side of the Pontiac. Now holding the shotgun only with his

right hand, Frago reached for the passenger door handle with his left hand. Twining suddenly burst from the car and shot Frago twice in the upper torso with a .357 magnum revolver, killing the officer as he dropped to the pavement. Gore's attention immediately went from Davis to Twining. The two exchanged gunfire, but neither hit his target. Davis then pulled his .38 caliber revolver from his waistband (the one he used earlier to threaten the driver of the southbound vehicle) and shot Gore twice in the chest, killing him instantly. It was now 11:55 pm, less than one minute after the stop.

Just one moment later, at 11:56 pm, a second CHP cruiser with troopers James Pence and George Alleyn arrived and parked on the left side of Gore and Frago's patrol car (see figure 4-2). Before the second patrol car came to a

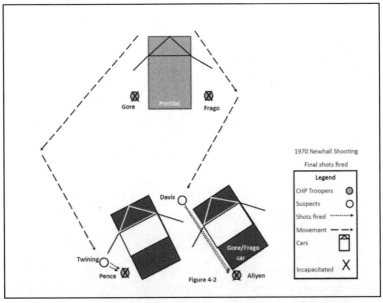

Figure 4-2

stop it started taking gunfire from Davis and Twining who had moved to the front of their Pontiac and were using it for cover. Alleyn exited the passenger's side of the patrol vehicle, shotgun in hand, and moved to the rear of Gore and Frago's car for cover. Pence bailed out of the driver's seat and took a position of cover behind the front left fender of his cruiser. Alleyn, still taking shots from the assailants, racked the shotgun twice, sending an unspent .12-gauge shell to the ground.

Pence and Alleyn began exchanging gunfire with Davis and Twining. Alleyn ran his shotgun dry and Davis, now armed with a shotgun of his own, advanced on Alleyn closing the distance. Alleyn responded shooting his revolver at Davis. Alleyn's shots went awry as Davis hit his mark. Meanwhile, Pence emptied his six-shot service revolver and was reloading when Twining rushed him. Twining executed Pence before he could finish reloading. It was now 11:58, four minutes after the initial stop—four officers lay dead.

During the mayhem a civilian witness, Gary Kness, came upon the shooting after Officers Pence and Alleyn were already engaged in the gunfight. Mr. Kness ran to assist the officers and was able to pick up Alleyn's revolver that lay next to his body and shoot at Davis. Davis received a minor non-life threatening wound from a bullet that likely ricocheted off the Pontiac. The second time Mr. Kness pulled the trigger the hammer fell on a spent cartridge. Out of ammunition and hearing sirens from other officers nearing the scene, Mr. Kness retreated to safety.

After murdering Pence and Alleyn, Davis and Twining returned to their car and fled. A short distance later they abandoned the car and retreated on foot. Twining, who had vowed never to return to prison, committed suicide. Davis was apprehended and sentenced to death, his sentence was later reduced to life in prison.[40] In 2009, Davis died behind bars of an apparent suicide. For an excellent detailed analysis of the shooting see *Newhall Shooting, A Tactical Analysis* by Mike Wood.

The tragic murder of four police officers in what became known as the "Newhall Incident" rocked the law enforcement community. For the first time in American history four law enforcement officers were slain in one incident. All four had been with the CHP for less than two years. Troopers Gore and Frago were 23; troopers Pence and Alleyn were 24. All were husbands and fathers. Although none of the officers were rookies, they were all rather new to the job, not long out of training. What went wrong? How could two ex-convicts outgun four trained professional police officers? The Newhall shooting caused police administrators to take a closer look at police training and their practices for preparing officers to fight with their guns.

Reality Based Training

The importance of training and preparation cannot be overstated. Professional athletes know the importance of proper preparation. The Golden State Warriors' guard Stephen Curry is one of National Basketball Association's (NBA) best jump-shooters. Curry led the Warriors to win the 2015 NBA World Championship and to start the next season with a best ever start for any team in the league's history. Curry's God-given abilities to perform under the stress of playing in high-pressure games before thousands of fans and millions of TV viewers are fine-tuned through training and preparing before game time.

In addition to his regular workout routine and team practices, Curry prepares physically and mentally on the

---

[40] (Wood, 2013)

court for 75 minutes prior to each game. In his pre-game routine, Curry practices jump shots from different places on the court while visualizing his opponent guarding him. Here's how a writer from the *New York Post* reported Curry's pre-game regimen at Brooklyn's Barclays Center, where Curry scored 11 of his 28 points in the third quarter to lead the Warriors to a victory over the Nets.

> Barclays Center turned into Steph World on Sunday night. And it was beautiful to see. This all started 75 minutes before the game. There was Stephen Curry going through his artistic pregame shooting routine, hitting jumpers from every angle on every spot on the floor as his side of the court was stuffed with onlookers.
>
> Curry was simply imagining what was to come later. When it was real, he did the exact same thing at the end of the third quarter as the guard exploded for 11 of the Warriors' final 13 points of the quarter.[41]

Curry knows that training and preparation aren't only for physical conditioning—they're also for mental conditioning. In the best way he can, Curry mimics real-life situations while making his shots. Curry understands his performance in a real game is directly related to this pre-game simulation. The result? Curry is the best in the game, and his team keeps on winning.

The Newhall shooting was the catalyst that transformed police training into what is now known as *Reality Based Training* (RBT). Reality Based Training seeks to mimic the real-life situations police officers face in the

---

[41] (Kernan, 2015)

course of their daily work. This is exactly what Stephen Curry does before each game. However, even during the most intense contest the worst thing Curry will ever face is losing a basketball game. A gunfight is different. Bill Jordan, retired Assistant Chief Patrol Inspector of the Border Patrol, titled his classic 1965 book about gunfights, *No Second Place Winner*. While the losers of a basketball game will live to play another game, a loser in a gunfight may not live to see another day. Jordan's book, directed at law enforcement, teaches officers how to prepare tactically to win a gunfight, not how to come in second.

There are two basic aspects to prepare for a gunfight, learning *how* to shoot and learning *when* to shoot. This means training must include both practical shooting techniques and real-life scenarios. Director of Training at Armiger Police Training Institute, Kenneth Murray, put it this way, "When learning how to fight with a pistol or a rifle, teaching a man *how to shoot* is vastly easier than teaching him *how to think* his way through a gunfight."[42]

> *"When learning how to fight with a pistol or a rifle, teaching a man* how to shoot *is vastly easier than teaching him* how to think *his way through a gunfight."*
> —Kenneth Murray

The proliferation of public shootings has caused many in private and public industry to at least think about their response to an active killer invading their building, event, or sanctuary. Some remain in denial while I've heard other leaders say things like, "I've got a couple guys who have their concealed carry permits. They'll take care of it." There's a false assumption that having a concealed carry permit qualifies someone to successfully win a gunfight. But the Newhall shooting taught us that even trained law enforce-

---

[42] (Murray K. R., 2004, p. 14)

46

ment professionals don't automatically hit what they're aiming at in a real combat situation. The four officers obviously passed all their department's required marksmanship training for revolvers and shotguns, but they were unprepared for using those skills during real-life engagement. The four officers in the Newhall shooting fired a total of 11 rounds from their revolvers with zero hits. Frago never got a shot off and Alleyn missed with his shotgun. A good question to ask is: Has the use of RBT in police training since 1970 helped achieve a better hit ratio?

For years researchers found that the hit ratio for officer-involved shootings was a miserable 15-25%. This suggests that under the pressure of real gunfire performance plummets.[43] That means that 75-85% of the time officers miss. However, Dr. Bill Lewinski, executive director of the Force Science Research Center at Minnesota State University-Mankato reports that a 2005 study by Firearms Trainer Tom Aveni shows actual hits for some agencies to be better. In one large, metropolitan agency the hit rate was 64% for daytime shootings and 45% for shootings occurring in low light (which includes inside lighting conditions). The study also revealed that hit counts went down when the number of shots fired went up and when more officers were involved in the shooting. One agency reported,

> [W]hen only one officer fired during an encounter, the average hit ratio was 51 percent. When an additional officer got involved in shooting, hits dropped dramatically, to 23 percent. With more than 2 officers shooting, the average hit ratio was only 9 percent.[44]

---

[43] (Lewinski, PoliceOne.com, 2005)
[44] (Lewinski, PoliceOne.com, 2005)

According to Aveni's research the numbers are better than originally thought. However, here's the reality: police officers involved in inside shootings still only have a hit rate of less than 50% in the best trained agencies, and this hit rate drops dramatically when more officers are involved. These are trained police officers. What hit ratio do you think civilians with little or no training will have? What or who will those bullets hit? This is why training is so critical.

While law enforcement officers only have about a 50% hit rate, the other 50% that miss their intended target rarely hit innocent victims—why? Training and preparation. One of the four basic firearms safety rules is to be aware of the target and beyond.[45]

Conclusion

Reality Based Training helps train and prepare officers for real-life gunfights. Anyone who arms themselves for self-protection, or protection of others, has the potential to be involved in a gunfight. Therefore, engaging in scenario training that mimics real-life incidents becomes a necessary part of RBT. Scenario-based training will help you quickly make the right decision in the heat of battle. Reality Based Training includes shooting-simulator training and scenario training with nonlethal training aids. However, in order to get the most out of RBT you need to be aware of the psychological and physiological changes you may experience during an actual gunfight.

---

[45] (The four basic rules are covered in chapter eight Firearms Basics)

The Implications of Being Involved in a Gunfight

Chapter 5

Farmer's Daughter Shooting

It was busier than usual on the evening of Thursday, March 17, 1988. I finished booking my prisoner into the downtown San Antonio jail and just after 9 pm I advised my dispatcher that I was back in service. I keyed the mic, "41-01, I'll be 10-8." On the way back to my patrol district I stopped by a Denny's restaurant hoping to grab a cup of coffee and finish up some reports. Before I reached the restaurant door, a call for a man with a gun came out in my district; the dispatcher called my number, "41-01, respond to the Farmer's Daughter for a man with a gun."

"Ten-four, 41-01, on the way," Officers Mike Lacy and Christine Kraeger volunteered to back me up. The Farmer's Daughter was an old-time Country and Western dance hall that catered to an older crowd. For the five years I worked the district I never had any trouble; in fact I can't recall ever being dispatched there for a disturbance. The dispatcher provided more information while I was enroute. She said a black male in a blue and white van was in the parking lot. He possibly had a gun.

49

Lacy, Kraeger, and I arrived at the same time. I went inside to contact the club's plain-clothes security guard who reported the incident. The security guard said a black male driving a blue and white van had pulled up to the front of the club almost driving into it. The guard saw what he believed was the butt of a handgun on the console between the van's front seats. He told the suspect to leave, but instead the man drove to the parking lot and parked. The guard pointed out where he believed the van was located. I radioed the other officers and we approached on foot.

The van was parked facing away from us. We walked closer and I could see someone sitting in the driver's seat— a black male. He looked over his right shoulder and saw me walking in his direction; he quickly ducked, lying down across the console, where the gun was said to be located. I alerted Lacy and Kraeger. Lacy had swung wide and was approaching the right-front while Kraeger and I continued to approach the right-rear of the van.

The suspect was still out of sight when I stopped behind the van. Moving to the left (driver's) side with my right hand on my service revolver and my flashlight in my left hand, I shined light into the cab, ordering the suspect to show me his hands. The suspect suddenly popped up. "Place both hands on the steering wheel," I ordered. He placed his left hand on the steering wheel and kept his right hand out of sight. I ordered him twice more to show me his hands as I continued walking slowly up to the driver's side. Keeping his attention on me, the suspect didn't see Lacy on the other side of the van; but Lacy was able to see inside the van. Lacy mouthed "He has a gun." I drew my revolver and took a step back.

The two parking spaces on the van's driver's side were empty. Directly behind and parked perpendicular to the van a Chevy El Camino was parked (see figure 5-1). I backed away and took a position on the opposite side of the El Camino. Kraeger was to my right. Lacy remained on the other side of the van. The suspect opened the driver's door and exited the van. Stepping away from the van he stood facing me. Both his hands were at his side and in his right hand was a small single-action pistol. I knew the hammer needed to be cocked before the pistol could be shot. Pointing my .357 magnum service revolver at him, I order him to drop the gun. He refused. With his right thumb he was attempting to cock the pistol.

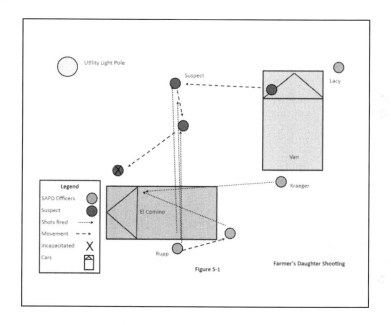

Figure 5-1

Thoughts raced through my mind. Things seemed to slow down. I was watching his hand with the gun in it, giving orders to drop it, and thinking about my wife Sherry all at the same time. We had been married less than two years. "Drop the gun!" I ordered. Ignoring my orders, he just looked at me with a blank stare. I pictured Chief Gibson driving up to my house to notify Sherry I'd been killed in the line-of-duty. He continued to stare. "Drop it, or I'll kill you!" I hoped the threat of death would get through to him. I could picture a hearse. Sherry dressed in black. People comforting her. He continued to stare. No! No, he wasn't going to do this to Sherry. His hand started to come up. I pulled the trigger, he staggered toward me, and again I fired. He continued to come. He was almost at the passenger side of the El Camino; his hands were still moving. Now he was moving to my left. *Bang!* Another shot. The man dropped on the opposite side of the El Camino. I moved around and found him lying on the ground.

Laying on his left side he was looking at his blood covered right hand and his index finger that was dangling by a piece of skin. I moved in, still pointing my revolver at him. "I can see his hands, find the gun," I said. Lacy located the gun. Kreager and Lacy were okay and none of us were shot. The threat was over. We sought to administer first aid while notifying the dispatcher that we had been involved in a shooting and needed paramedics. Emergency Medical Services (EMS) transported the suspect to the hospital. Several hours later he was pronounced dead.

It was over. Or was it? What happens after the smoke clears? What are the after effects of being involved in a shooting? I had just killed a man, what now?

Immediately after the shooting I had trouble putting the whole event together. I didn't know how many times I shot; I thought I shot once or twice—maybe. Checking my cylinder, to my surprise, I found four spent cartridges. Four shots, did I even hit him? Was it Kreager or Lacy who shot him? We had department issued Smith and Wesson, model 65, .357 magnum revolvers and I didn't recall hearing any shots. There was no ringing in my ears. Where did my flashlight go? I remember having it when I walked up to the van, but I don't remember what I did with it. Looking around, I found it had rolled under the van. I must have dropped it when I drew my revolver, but I didn't remember doing so.

The follow-up investigation showed a clear picture. My first shot hit the suspect's right hand, the hand that held the pistol. Later, I found it's not uncommon for police officers to shoot a gun because that is where they are focusing. My second shot hit him in the middle of his chest, the third shot passed through the passenger side bed of the El Camino and into his right leg. The fourth shot hit the rear glass of the El Camino. With the fourth shot I was tracking him as he moved to my left. Kraeger shot once, not hitting the suspect, Lacy didn't have a clear shot and didn't shoot from the other side of the van. I'd shot plenty of times on the range, but this wasn't a paper target. I'd hunted and killed birds, squirrels, and deer, but this wasn't an animal. This was different—this was a human being.

Perceptual Distortions

During high-stress situations (such as deadly encounters) humans experience perceptual distortions. Perceptual distortions affect the way things are *perceived*. A distortion means things are perceived other than as they are in reality. Perceptual distortions include hearing, vision, automatic responses, timing, freezing, and distracting thoughts. In some cases these perceptual distortions can cause the "fright" or the "numb-and-dumb" response of doing nothing, and/or other negative responses. But in other cases the distortions can produce positive sensory responses.

Dr. Alexis Artwohl has done extensive research on officer-involved shootings and how highly emotional experiences (i.e. being involved in a gunfight) impact perception and memory.[46] Many officers reported experiencing several perception or memory changes during a single event. See table 1 for her findings.

Training for a gunfight includes knowing to expect sensory distortion during a deadly encounter. There are both

---

[46] (Artwohl, 2002, pp. 18-24)

positive perceptions and negative perceptions you may experience when engaged in deadly combat. While not everyone will experience every distortion, most will experience one or more. Dave Grossman has done extensive study on

---

Perceptual Distortions

From *Perceptual and Memory Distortion During Officer-Involved Shootings*
By Dr. Alexis Artwohl
FBI Law Enforcement Bulletin
October 2002

- 84% heard sounds diminished
- 16% heard sounds intensified
- 79% experienced tunnel vision
- 71% experienced greater visual clarity
- 62% experienced slow motion time
- 17% experienced fast motion time
- 74% responded on "automatic pilot"
- 52% reported memory loss for part of the event
- 46% reported memory loss for part of their own behavior
- 21% reported memory distortion
- 39% experienced dissociation (i.e. a sense of detachment)
- 26% experienced intrusive distracting thoughts
- 7% reported temporary paralysis

Table 1

---

perceptual distortions. I experienced perceptual distortion in the Farmer's Daughter shooting detailed above.

At the time of the shooting I wasn't familiar with Grossman's research. However, after hearing his *Bullet Proof Mind* seminar, I was an immediate fan. Eight years after the shooting I got answers to questions and was able to better understand the dynamics of a gunfight.

Grossman admits there's a lot more research that needs to be done, but the current understanding is that changes to sensory organs are side effects of vasocon-striction.[47] For a more detailed discussion see his book *On Combat*. Below I will share how just a few of Dr. Artwohl's noted perceptual distortions affected me, personally.

Hearing and Seeing Distortions

A four-inch .357 magnum revolver makes a lot of noise. Why then did I not hear five full-powered magnum rounds go off during the Farmer's Daughter shooting? Because I experienced *auditory exclusion*. Auditory exclusion is more than simply not hearing something because your attention is elsewhere. We've all experienced times when we didn't hear our name being called because we were captivated by a movie we were watching, a book we were reading, or when we were in an intense conversation with someone else. Auditory exclusion is not simply being distracted.

Dr. Artwohl calls this phenomenon *diminished sound* and describes it as, "…the inability to hear very loud sounds that a person ordinarily obviously would hear, such as gunshots. It ranges from not hearing these sounds at all to hearing them in an odd muffled, distant manner."[48] Auditory exclusion is a *distortion*. In reality, there was a loud noise, but you didn't hear it, or it was significantly diminished. Grossman explains,

> Not seeing or hearing something because you are concentrating on something else is a psychological manifestation. Whereas "tunnel vision" and "auditory exclusion" appear to involve both psychological "concentration" influences and powerful physiological effects

---

[47] (Grossman, On Combat, 2008, p. 54)
[48] (Artwohl, 2002, p. 20)

caused by biomechanical changes to the eye and ear.[49]

Dr. Lewinski defines biomechanics as "the mechanics of biological and muscular activity."[50] Biomechanics are effected by either external or internal forces physically acting upon the body. In the instance of auditory exclusion there are internal factors that somehow either completely shut down or greatly muffle the report of the gunshot. Grossman terms this Type-1 Auditory Exclusion:

> The auditory system appears to "blink" creating a biomechanical shutdown that protects the ears from ringing afterwards. However…Type-I Auditory Exclusion…does not happen when you are under the stress of competitive shooting. It only happens in the actual killing circumstances of recreational hunting and combat.[51]

This explains why I didn't hear the shots and felt no effects (i.e. ringing in my ears) of them afterwards. Why is it important to know this? It's important to understand that auditory exclusion is a common phenomenon in a gunfight and shouldn't take you by surprise. Some police officers report not hearing their own gunshots or those of their partner's and believing their guns were either malfunctioning or their partner wasn't shooting.[52]

There's another type of auditory exclusion, which Grossman dubs Type-II. "Type-II Auditory Exclusion can

---

[49] (Grossman, On Combat, 2008, p. 54)
[50] (Lewinski, Biomechanics of Lethal Force Encounters--Officer Movements, 2002, p. 19)
[51] (Grossman, On Combat, 2008, p. 61)
[52] (Grossman, On Combat, 2008, p. 56)

happen when you are completely relaxed (i.e. not in an excited state) and appears to be a result of the body receiving two simultaneous and overwhelming sensory stimuli." This may explain why some people who witness a shooting say the shots sounded like a "popping sound." The stimulus of seeing (visual sensory) someone being shot overwhelms, overloads, and blocks out or diminishes hearing (audio sensory).

On the other side of the coin, there are intensified sounds where the gunshots are extremely loud and other senses shut down. "The eyes turn off, the ears turn on and, as one law enforcement trainer put it, 'You hunker down and die, blind and afraid.'"[53] That's not an appropriate response.

As mentioned in an above quote, *tunnel vision* is also common. Tunnel vision is the mind focusing so intently on one object that nothing else is seen. Think about closing one eye and with the other looking through a paper-towel tube. All you can see is where you are pointing the tube, that's tunnel vision. In gunfights it's common for officers to focus so intently on the threat (i.e. the gun) nothing else is seen. This is not necessarily ideal since there may be more than one aggressor or one aggressor may have more than one weapon. What if your focus is on a knife in one hand and you don't see a gun in the other?

Understanding tunnel vision is important; proper training can help eliminate it. Police firearms instructors are teaching "scan-down-scan."[54] Scan-down-scan or "scanning" is an exercise in which officers break their focus on the target and scan to the left and right, then "check their six" by looking behind them immediately after shooting each stage of the course-of-fire. The hope is, that in an actual gunfight officers will avoid or break tunnel vision by scanning for other threats.

---

[53] (Grossman, On Combat, 2008, p. 62)
[54] We started teaching "scan-down-scan" at the San Antonio Police training academy in the 1990s.

Further, keep in mind the bad guy may also be experiencing tunnel vision when he suddenly realizes he's facing armed opposition. Dr. Artwohl's research revealed 8 out of 10 police officers had experienced tunnel vision[55] so it's highly probable the aggressor is experiencing it as well. Police officers are taught to sidestep either right or left in a gunfight. This allows the officer to step "out of the sight" of a gunman who is experiencing tunnel vision (and even if the gunman isn't experiencing tunnel vision, he now has a moving target).

Dr. Artwohl's study also revealed that some officers experienced a heightened sense of hearing and/or vision that were considered positive effects. It seems during times of emergency survival senses that are needed somehow intensify providing, for example, better hearing or seeing as the situation dictates. One officer reported that while the sound of the gunshots diminished he was able to hear the footsteps of his assailant.[56] Know that you may experience a heightened sense of hearing or seeing; that's good; use it to your advantage.

Automatic Responses

Why did I shoot four times? Because of training. The police firearms instructors taught me to shoot until the threat was over. One firearms instructor drilled into our heads, "Shoot until he stops doing what it was that caused you to start shooting." I shot until the threat was over. When I perceived no more threat, I stopped shooting. This is described as "automatic pilot." Automatic pilot is responding to stimuli with no conscious thought of what actions to take, you simply respond. It's like when you're driving and a child runs into the street, your right foot immediately goes from

---

[55] (Artwohl, 2002, p. 20)
[56] (Grossman, On Combat, 2008, p. 64)

the accelerator pedal to the brake pedal without conscious thought. How many times have you stopped your car by removing your foot from the accelerator pedal and pressing the brake pedal? Each time you do so you are training your foot and leg what to do in an emergency. When the emergency arises, you respond. One's response in a gunfight is directly related to training.

After the Newhall shooting (discussed in chapter four) the California Highway Patrol (CHP) changed their firearms and tactics training. One of the changes they made was removing cans from the range that were used to collect spent shell casings. In an effort to save clean-up time and keep the pistol range looking neat and tidy, during the course-of-fire students would carefully empty their spent casings from their revolver into a can before reloading.[57] So what's the big deal? Muscle memory (although technically muscles don't have memory). Any athlete is familiar with muscle memory training. Quarterbacks and receivers practice the same routes over and over. Basketball players practice free-throws over and over. Golfers practice their swing over and over. What you do in training is what you'll do when it counts the most. In the heat of battle is when the forebrain shuts down and the midbrain takes over—you operate on auto-pilot.[58] If the wrong thing is in your midbrain things go downhill, fast. Rather than drawing from muscle memory that will bring a quick and positive end to the event, your actions (or inactions) may very well lead to a less than desirable end.

> *What you do in training is what you'll do when it counts the most.*

This is why training and practice is critical. It's been said, "Practice doesn't make perfect; perfect practice makes

---

[57] (Wood, 2013, p. 103)
[58] (Grossman, On Combat, 2008, p. 75)

perfect." The point being practice right so you will respond right. What you do in training and practice is what you'll do in an actual situation. In a study of the dynamics of biomechanics in officer-involved-shootings, Dr. Lewinski found, "the greatest factor in the speed of the draw is the amount of time the officer spends practicing."[59]

Time Distortions

Time distortions can manifest themselves by either slow-motion or fast-motion time. In the Farmer's Daughter shooting I experienced slow-motion time. As the suspect exited the van and stepped facing me it seemed like forever, while in reality the whole incident was over very quickly. Not expecting this, I actually remember becoming fatigued (or at least feeling I was fatigued) as we faced off and I was ordering him to drop his gun.

Former football running back for the Los Angeles Raiders, Marcus Allen, described a moment of slow-motion time he experienced in his famous Super Bowl XVIII 74-yard touchdown run. Allen said during the run everything seemed to slow down and he had all the time he needed to dodge defenders. Then twenty yards from the end zone, when the "threat" was over, his perception returned to regular speed.[60]

Slow-motion time is a good thing, but you need to be aware it may occur. If it does, use it to your advantage. Our brains are capable of processing information at speeds we can't fathom.

Fast-motion time isn't good. This is when things seem to be going so fast we don't have time to react. We are behind the curve and frantically trying to catch-up as we process what is happening. Fast-motion time is a result of being

---

[59] (Lewinski, Biomechanics of Lethal Force Encounters--Officer Movements, 2002, p. 20)
[60] (ESPN Sports, 2012)

unprepared to respond in an appropriate way (lack of proper training) and/or being taken by surprise, such as being caught in what is known as Condition White, one of four conditions discussed in chapter six. While your mind is processing, "There's a man with a gun and he's pointing it at me (or another innocent person). That's not right." The aggressor is already shooting even as your mind is telling you, "You have a gun. You have been trained. Respond." If, on the other hand, you are in Condition Yellow, being aware and half-expecting something might happen, then when you see the man with the gun your mind says, "Man with a gun. Respond." And you do, like stepping on the brake pedal.

Freezing or temporary paralysis

Freezing or *temporary paralysis* is cognitively coming to a stop and being unable to function. It's the "numb-and-dumb" response, and clearly ineffectual. When our response is no response, we have shut down completely.

> [S]ome officers perform poorly in combat because they are victims of uncontrollable physiological changes in their bodies. These changes can alter or shut down some cognitive processes entirely, can make them freeze in place when they should be moving, and can also dramatically impact basic senses like sight and sound, which can corrupt or block the information an officer needs to make proper and timely decisions and take precise actions.[61]

While freezing seems to be a death note, there is some good news. In Dr. Artwohl's study only seven percent

---

[61] (Wood, 2013, p. 121)

of officers experienced freezing or *temporary paralysis.* That tells us that when someone is trained and prepared there's a 93 percent chance they will not experience temporary paralysis. But there's more good news. She discovered that often the freezing is for a very short time. Dr. Artwohl, "…found that, in fact, this was simply the normal 'action-reaction' gap that occurs because the officers can shoot only after the suspect has engaged in behavior that represents a threat."[62]

Distracting Thoughts

In Dr. Artwohl's study, she reports that 26 percent of the officers involved in a gunfight had *intrusive distracting thoughts.* She defines intrusive distracting thoughts as, "those not immediately relevant to the tactical situation, often including thoughts about loved ones or personal matters."[63] On their face, intrusive thoughts appear to be negative. Dr. Artwohl even defines them with two adjectives: *intrusive distracting* thoughts. But, I suggest the two adjectives can be separated. In other words, *intrusive* thoughts are not necessarily *distracting* thoughts. How long does a thought take? What kind of thought is it? In my case the intrusive thoughts about my wife weren't distracting, in fact, I believe they spurred me on to make the right decision. During the Farmer's Daughter shooting, I experienced intrusive thoughts about San Antonio Police Chief Gibson going to my house and telling Sherry I'd been killed in the line-of-duty. Chief Gibson never made that trip to my house. Sherry and I now have three children and several grandchildren. None of whom may have ever been born if I hesitated.

Grossman's research supports my thoughts,

---

[62] (Artwohl, 2002, p. 21)
[63] (Artwohl, 2002, p. 21)

In the heat of battle, many warriors think of their family. One police officer said that during a gunfight, he had a vision of his three-year-old boy…. These intrusive thoughts are not always distracting, sometimes they can serve as an inspiration or motivation…. He [the officer] says that a sudden thought about his young son motivated him to get up [after being shot in the face] and return fire, killing his assailant.[64]

While the cause of these sensory distortions aren't fully understood we understand they happen during deadly combat incidents, when we are in a heightened state of emotional arousal. Dr. Artwohl's research noted that neither she nor others conducting similar studies measured other distortions such as distance, color, face recognition, or lighting distortions. When fighting for survival strange things happen to our bodies. These changes are both physiological and perceptual. Some are beneficial and some are detrimental to our survival and a successful outcome. Training and preparation will help overcome the negative effects and help us take advantage of the positive effects.

Picking up the Pieces

Not only do we need to be aware of the physiological and perceptual distortions during the heat of battle, we need to be aware of them when we are trying to pick up the pieces after the smoke clears. Likely you won't recall everything after the event for some time, if ever. Dr. Artwohl found that "…the body of research on perception and memory supports

---

[64] (Grossman, On Combat, 2008, p. 99)

the fact that people rarely are capable of total and perfect recall of events."[65]

It is important to understand that if you are involved in a gunfight you will likely have memory gaps. While there are certain things that are "burned into" your memory, there are other things you just won't recall. The follow-up investigation by law enforcement will help to fill in the gaps, but understand you may not be privy to this information for some time.

In his book *On Killing,* Grossman asked the question, "What does it feel like to kill?" He answers with five basic stages to killing: (1) the concern stage, (2) the actual kill, (3) exhilaration, (4) remorse, and (5) rationalization and acceptance.[66] In stage one, *the concern stage,* you wonder if you will be able to respond properly at the moment of truth. If you are honest with your willingness to pull the trigger coupled with proper training and preparation be

> *Five basic stages to killing: (1) the concern stage, (2) the actual kill, (3) exhilaration, (4) remorse, and (5) rationalization and acceptance.*
> —Dave Grossman

confident that you will respond properly in the heat of battle. Stage two, *the actual kill,* is "simply" applying your training at the moment of truth and knowing that the goal isn't to kill, but to stop. Stage three, *exhilaration,* may not be experienced by everyone. Exhilaration is experienced because you won. You were just in a gunfight and you survived. I experienced this immediately after the Farmer's Daughter shooting. It helped that no innocent persons were hurt or killed. Nevertheless, I felt guilty about feeling good. At the time I didn't know this was a "normal" and acceptable response.

---

[65] (Artwohl, 2002, p. 18)
[66] (Grossman, On Killing, 1996, pp. 231-240)

Stage four, *remorse*, may also not be experienced by everyone. At the risk of not being thought of as a caring Christian, I never felt remorse. I was more pragmatic after the shooting—realizing he was attempting to shoot me; I shot him first.

The fifth stage is critical, *rationalization and acceptance*. This is where you understand the necessity for doing what you did and accept it. If someone appears capable, has the means and the opportunity, and threatens to kill or cause serious bodily injury to an innocent person, then he is responsible for what happens to him. Remember the lists of warriors in the Bible? These men are forever memorialized by the Lord in his holy Word for their willingness to stop bad people by killing them, thus stopping them from killing others.

Family members and friends will be interested in what happened. They'll want to know all the details. Now is the time to explain to your spouse, clergy, parents, or closest friend what to expect if you are involved in a shooting. Sharing is important, but you need to share with those who will not question or judge your actions. "Why didn't you shoot him in the leg?" "Why didn't you tell him to drop the gun?" Why questions are not what you need. You'll need to share with trusted others, and hopefully they will be familiar with what you are going through (share this book with them *before* something happens).

If you are a family member, friend, or clergy of a person involved in a deadly force encounter, please recognize their need for support. A safe person to talk with may also be needed. Let them tell you as much as they would like to share. Realize they may be feeling guilty, especially if others were harmed or killed. This "survivor's guilt" is normal. Encourage them and give them permission not to feel guilty. They responded as best they could and survived. There's no reason to feel guilty about winning a gun battle. Your affirmation is vital!

Use of Force policy/Federal and State law

Federal law is governed by the US Constitution, and the Second Amendment says,

> A well regulated Militia, being necessary to the security of a free State, the right of the people to keep and bear Arms, shall not be infringed.

Many believe it is the government's responsibility to protect us. By passing the Second Amendment the government acknowledged its inability to adequately protect each individual and has given us the responsibility and authority to protect ourselves.

Lethal use of force laws in defense of life varies from state to state. However, most are generally the same: deadly force is justified to stop the imminent and unlawful use of deadly force, or force that would cause serious bodily harm against an innocent person. That innocent person can be the person using the deadly force (i.e. you) against the aggressor or another person (i.e. a family member or other innocent person).

According to the FBI website,

> FBI special agents may use deadly force only when necessary—when the agent has a reasonable belief that the subject of such force poses an imminent danger of death or serious physical injury to the agent or another person. If feasible, a verbal warning to submit to the authority of the special agent is given prior to the use of deadly force.[67]

---

[67] (The Federal Bureau of Investigation, 2015)

Notice the FBI use of force requires the agent to have "a reasonable belief" that the danger is "imminent." Both reasonable belief and imminent danger must be present. Someone standing up in the middle of a church service and yelling, "I hate God and all you people" isn't putting people in imminent peril. However, that same person standing up and yelling, "I hate God and all you people" while brandishing a gun would be perceived as putting people in imminent peril. One key in self-defense laws is that of reasonableness. The person using deadly force in self-defense or defense of another must be acting reasonably. This means the fear of great harm or imminent death that you experience must be sufficient enough to cause a *reasonable* person in the same or similar circumstances to feel that same fear; and that fear would cause a reasonable person to use deadly force. Further, you must act on the imminent fear alone, not on anger or revenge.

Consult your state penal code for the laws governing where you live. If you look for the information from the internet make sure you are on your state's website. Most will have a "dot-gov" ending such as "Idaho.gov". The state law of Idaho that deals with legal jeopardy reads as follows:

> 19-202A. Legal jeopardy in cases of self-defense and defense of other threatened parties.
>
> No person in this state shall be placed in legal jeopardy of any kind whatsoever for protecting himself or his family by reasonable means necessary, or when coming to the aid of another whom he reasonably believes to be in imminent danger of or the victim of aggravated assault, robbery, rape, murder or other heinous crime.

Once the "imminent danger" is over there's no further justification for the use of force. For example, if the aggressor throws his gun to the ground, holds his hands in a surrender position, and says, "I give up," then although you had justification to shoot moments before (and may have), the threat of death and/or serious bodily injury is over, as well as the justification for using deadly force.

Criminal investigation

When shots are fired the police are called. If you're involved in a shooting and law enforcement has not been contacted, ensure they are notified immediately. Understand that if you shoot someone (or at someone), there will be a criminal investigation to determine what crimes were committed and who violated the law. If you are a police officer, there will also be an internal investigation to determine if department policies or procedures were violated and the same applies to private security. Criminal (and internal) investigations can be both intimidating and stressful, but knowing what to expect will help relieve some of that stress.

Procedures vary but most law enforcement agencies have similar guidelines for handling officer-involved shootings. If you are an officer or work for a private agency, be familiar with your agency's guidelines. Generally, the criminal and internal investigations will be separate. The homicide unit or a special detail that may consist of officers from outside agencies will conduct the criminal investigation. For police, the internal administrative investigation will be conducted under the direction of the head of the agency or a person designated to act on their behalf. Also know that the Federal Bureau of Investigation (FBI) may be asked to investigate if there are allegations of civil rights violations by law enforcement officers.

It's important to know that when the police are responding to a shooting they usually do not know the good guys from the bad guys. Make sure you listen and obey what they tell you. Understand that you very well may be told to put your hands up, lie down prone on the ground, and quite possibly even be handcuffed. Yes, you can be handcuffed and not arrested. The officers' job is to ensure the safety of everyone on scene and until things can be sorted out you may be "treated like a criminal."

After the scene is safe and the injured are receiving medical treatment, officers will secure the scene and separate witnesses. Part of securing the scene is collecting evidence, which includes your gun. You'll likely be placed in a police vehicle and transported to another location to provide a statement—this doesn't mean you are under arrest. The reason for separating witnesses is to prevent them from collaborating or unintentionally influencing each other. If the police suspect that you have violated the law you will be read the *Miranda* warning and afforded the opportunity to secure a lawyer prior to answering any questions. If the police have probable cause to believe you committed a crime, you will likely be booked into jail and required to post bail to be released.

Shooting scenes are diverse and complicated, but there are three basic things investigators are looking for in a justified use of deadly force case: *ability, opportunity,* and *jeopardy.*

Ability

First, the attacker must have the *ability* to cause harm to you or another. Several factors may be taken into account: Was the assailant armed with a deadly weapon (e.g. a gun, knife)? Was he armed with another instrument that may not be designed as a weapon (e.g. a baseball bat, tire iron, or screwdriver) but is nevertheless capable of causing serious bodily injury or death? Ability also includes physical ability. A large man may very well have the ability to cause serious bodily injury or death to a smaller man or woman with his bare hands. Simply put, the assailant must be *able* to carry out serious bodily injury or death.

Opportunity

Second, the attacker must have the *opportunity* to cause harm to you or another. Opportunity is tied to time and place or proximity. At this *time* and in this *place* does the attacker have the ability to do harm? In other words, is the threat of harm imminent? A would-be assailant armed with a knife that calls from a distant location does not pose an imminent threat. Therefore, one would not be justified to drive to the person's location and shoot him. In this case, the proper course of action is to call the police and make a report. In fact, whenever it is possible, the best course of action is to make a police report when you face a real threat of harm.

Jeopardy

Third, the attacker must put you or another person in *jeopardy, i.e. real danger*. This, of course, is subjective. What you consider a real danger and what the police consider a real danger may be two different things. The police must try to get inside your head and determine what was going through your mind at the time of the shooting. Were your actions based on fear or revenge? Did you shoot because you were scared for your life or meting out your own justice?

The standard the courts apply is known as the *reasonable person standard*. The question the judge or jury will consider, and the police seek to determine, is if your actions were that of a *reasonable person* in the same or similar circumstances. A *reasonable person* is legally defined as "a hypothetical person in society who exercises average care, skill, and judgment in conduct and who serves as a comparative standard for determining liability." [68] If you are a police officer, your actions must be the same or similar to those of the hypothetical standard of a police officer in the same of similar circumstances.

Hence, the bottom line is that your decision to use deadly force must be against a person who: (1) has the *ability* to do serious bodily injury to you or another; (2) has the *opportunity* to do the harm; and (3) places you or another in imminent *jeopardy*.

Civil liabilities

What about the civil liabilities? Can you be sued for using deadly force? Yes. Even deadly force deemed justified by a criminal court? Yes. A person can be sued at just about any time for anything. We've all heard about the often ridiculous lawsuits that tie up the courts, yet we continue to be involved in activities that we may be sued for—driving, working, owning a home, etc. While we may take precautions, we don't radically change what we do day-to-day because we fear being sued. I'll protect my family from an intruder coming into my home and I won't worry about being sued. The way to avoid successful litigation is to be properly trained, prepared, equipped, and act as a reasonable person would act given the same set of circumstances.

> The way to avoid successful litigation is to be properly trained, prepared, equipped, and act as a reasonable person would act given the same set of circumstances.

---

[68] (Farlex Legal Dictionary, N.D.)

Conditions for Battle

Chapter 6

The Church's Chicken Murders

In the spring of 1991, I was assigned to San Antonio's east side working a 5 pm to 3 am patrol shift. On April 18th, at about 1 am, I was dispatched to an apartment complex for a family disturbance. The dispatcher said the complainant's boyfriend was at the location and was threatening to shoot her. Officer Bob Bettis volunteered to back me up; minutes later Bettis and I arrived and located the apartment. Barbara, the complainant, said her boyfriend, Leander Floyd Jr., had just left on foot armed with two handguns. I radioed a description of Floyd over the police radio and warned that he was armed. Bettis and I searched, but were unable to locate him. Returning to the apartment, I told Barbara we couldn't find Floyd. Barbara decided to leave and stay with her mother. After seeing Barbara safely away, Bettis and I returned to service. At 3 am our shift ended.

Fourteen hours later, at 5 pm, on April 18th, 1991, Bettis and I were at roll-call. We figured it to be a busy night; so right after roll call we decided to grab a cup of coffee and something to eat. We went to the Iron Skillet restaurant, sat down and ordered. Moments later the police emergency tone sounded over our radios followed by the most unsettling thing a police officer can hear, *"Shots fired! Officer down."*

Twenty-six year old uniformed Officer Doug Goeble was eating at a Church's Chicken restaurant. Doug recently asked for his girlfriend's hand in marriage and was looking at wedding ring advertisements while he ate. Outside in the parking lot Floyd and Barbara were arguing. Doug didn't notice the disturbance—he was in Condition White described below. Floyd entered the restaurant, walked up behind Doug and shot him in the back of the head. Barbara ran into the restaurant hoping to find help. As Floyd was leaving he turned and shot Barbara several times in the back and fled on foot. I arrived to find both Doug and Barbara lying face down on the floor in pools of their own blood. Barbara was pronounced dead at the scene. Emergency Medical Technicians transported Doug to the hospital where he died two days later. Hours after the shooting, Floyd was apprehended. He received a life sentence for the two murders and remains in the custody of the Texas Department of Corrections.

The Mind Matters

Most police departments require officers to qualify with their handguns annually (and in some agencies more often). The typical course-of-fire consists of shooting at paper targets from various distances generally ranging from 3 to 25 yards. At each stage officers are told the number of rounds to shoot, the time limit, and if they must perform a reload or clear a malfunction. In the days before the Newhall shooting, that was about it. If officers could demonstrate the ability to punch a predetermined number of holes in a paper target that wasn't moving or shooting back, then they were good to go. And go they did. Right into gunfights that ended with officers missing their targets more often than hitting them, or even worse being killed. Clearly the officers were physically prepared; on the gun range they demonstrated the skill to shoot and hit what they were shooting. But that's only half the battle. The other half is between the ears—mental preparation. Bill Jordan writes, "Almost invariably a man, provided he does not have too much time to think, will automatically do what he has been trained to do. Again provided that his training has been thorough and intensive."[69]

> *"Almost invariably a man...will automatically do what he has been trained to do."*
> —Bill Jordan

Therefore, Reality Based Training must begin with an understanding of basic physiological conditions that may affect performance during a real gunfight. Just as athletes mentally prepare before a game, so too must those who choose to carry a gun to protect others prepare for genuine threats. Furthermore, athletes also understand that they must mentally stay in the game. Anyone who watches sporting events understands this important concept. Not staying mentally focused is why teams blow big leads. As the late Yogi Berra quipped, "Baseball is 90% mental, the other half physical." While we chuckle, the Hall of Fame player and long-time coach made his point. Mental preparation is key to being a winner.

There are different "mental conditions" we can be in at any one time. Those who've had the pleasures of raising children know the difference between hearing and listening. When my children were in their teens I'd often give them instructions, to which they acknowledged with a nod of the head and maybe even a "Yes, sir." But, in reality they were oblivious to what I said. They heard, but they weren't aware. In the *Basic Personal Protection in the Home Course* the National Rifle Association (NRA) refers to these conditions as *levels of awareness*. The NRA teaches four basic levels:

- Unaware

---

[69] (Jordan, 1965, p. 105)

- Aware
- Alert
- Alarm[70]

In the *unaware* level we are unconscious of our surroundings. This occurs when we are involved in an activity that occupies our mind. It doesn't take much to occupy the mind. It could be watching TV, talking, reading, etc. For my teenagers it was whatever they were doing other than paying attention to my instructions. The second level, *aware,* is described as being aware of our surroundings while remaining engaged in other activities. As you read this book you are still maintaining a level of consciousness in respect to your surroundings. It's possible to listen to the radio, be engaged in conversation, or cook while being conscious of your surroundings. The third level, *alert,* is a heightened state of awareness. For example, when there's a potential threat and your focus is on that possible danger. The fourth level, *alarm,* is your mental state when an aggressor is actively threatening or attacking you or another.

In his book *On Combat,* Dave Grossman uses colors to explain in even greater detail what the NRA calls levels of awareness. He describes possible mental conditions as follows:

- White
- Yellow
- Red
- Black.[71]

[70] (The National Rifle Association, 2012, pp. I-6)
[71] (Grossman, On Combat, 2008, pp. 30-49)

Condition White

In **Condition White** you are unprepared to engage in a gunfight. Like the *unaware* condition you are oblivious to any threat or imminent attack. Condition White is unacceptable for any on-duty police officer. Officer Goeble was a fine officer and was known to remain tactically aware. However, it was clear he was distracted by the excitement of his recent engagement.

Condition White is okay when in a safe place and not armed. Condition White is for home, play, and entertainment. Most Americans live in Condition White. The vast majority of people are oblivious to their surroundings. Not long ago I went out to eat with a friend. At the restaurant I noticed a man at a table twenty feet away who had a holstered pistol on his side in plain sight (Idaho is an open-carry state). It wasn't a small pistol; it was a full-sized Glock. Later, I asked my friend if he saw the man with the gun in the restaurant. He never noticed the man—Condition White.

Grossman says Condition White is for the protected, not the protector. Anyone armed to protect themselves and/or others needs to remain vigilant. This doesn't mean you need to be callous or unfriendly constantly walking around suspicious of everyone. It means you need to remain aware of your surroundings and be aware of people or things that are out of place, seem odd, or may pose a threat; this is called Condition Yellow.

Condition Yellow

Condition Yellow is the next step up the ladder of mental preparedness. The main difference between Condition White and Condition Yellow is psychological, not physiological—it's being mentally in the game. Grossman describes, "When you move up to a level of basic alertness and readiness, a place where you are psychologically prepared for combat, you have entered the realm of 'Condition Yellow.'"[72] Most people will never notice a person in Condition Yellow. In fact, those likely to notice are only others trained to be aware and those who know a person best.

When my wife Sherry and I first started dating she thought I wasn't interested in her—furthest thing from the truth. She felt this way because when we were in public she noticed my attention was split. While I paid attention to her, she also noticed I was always looking around. Only later did she realize it was second nature for me to be aware of my surroundings and the people in them. I learned the importance of this early on in my police career. Soon after becoming a police officer I was attending classes at San Antonio College, a large community college near downtown San Antonio. One morning as I was walking across the campus I heard someone yelling, "Officer Rupp, Officer Rupp!" Looking up to a second floor landing of an outside staircase I saw a young man waving at me, "Don't you remember me? You arrested me!" To be quite honest, I hadn't remembered him. But had I been in Condition Yellow I would have recognized his preoccupation with me. This was an early lesson for me to always be aware of my surroundings when in public.

Condition Yellow means being mentally in the game. Being aware of your surroundings and continually assessing potential threats. Colonel Jeff Cooper observes, "The great majority of victims of violent crime are taken by surprise. The one who anticipates the action wins."[73]

> "The great majority of victims of violent crime are taken by surprise. The one who anticipates the action wins."
> —Colonel Jeff Cooper

---

[72] (Grossman, On Combat, 2008, p. 30)
[73] (Cooper, 1972, p. 24)

Condition Yellow means facing the direction that's most likely to pose a threat. If you are in a restaurant, then position yourself so you can observe people coming and going. Try to select a table where you can watch the cash register and/or the front door. When inside a public building (e.g. church, department store, or mall), stand facing the entrances. You may choose a side wall to back-up against in order to see people entering and exiting the building. Keep a clear path between you and the most likely place from which a threat will come. In other words, don't allow family members between you and a potential threat.

Condition Yellow means to look for things that are out of place, such as someone wearing an overcoat on a warm day, a young man coming to church by himself, a car backing into a stall rather than pulling straight in, or parking in a way that just doesn't seem right. Things that may seem innocent (and very well may be) should grab your attention because they're unusual.

In *Left of Bang* Patrick Van Horne and Jason Riley write about combat profiling. Combat profiling is a program designed to keep Marines on patrol in war zones alive. America's enemies don't play by the Geneva Conventions' rules of engagement. One rule of theirs is "Parties to a conflict shall at all times distinguish between the civilian population and combatants in order to spare civilian population and property."[74] Hence, our marines and soldiers have the task of distinguishing between good guys and bad guys who all look alike. Combat profiling teaches marines to recognize things that are abnormal, make a quick assessment of a potential threat, and take appropriate action. How does this work in a foreign culture and environment? The same way it works in a familiar culture and environment. It starts with establishing a baseline of behavior and then taking note of anomalies—something either above or below the baseline.

---

[74] (International Committee of the Red Cross, 1988)

Condition Yellow works the same way. First a baseline needs to be established. A baseline is "normal" behavior for people in a given environment. Think of a man in a grocery store. What would be a baseline? It's normal behavior to push a shopping cart, or grab a grocery basket with his sunglasses resting on top of his head when he enters the store. It's also normal to look at a piece of paper or on his smart phone (perhaps he's looking at a list of items he needs). Looking at the signs above the aisles that list the items stocked there is normal behavior. If you were in a grocery store and saw a man fitting the above profile there would be no cause for alarm. With practice you could easily take all this information in with a quick glance.

However, if you saw that same man enter the store wearing his sunglasses or cap pulled down as he passed by the shopping carts and baskets you should take note. Perhaps you also notice he keeps his right hand hidden from sight in the front pocket of his hoodie. "Why a hoodie?" you ask yourself, it's a warm summer day. Rather than looking at the signs above the aisles he seems to be looking at people. And rather than head for the groceries he's heading directly for a cash register.

In their book, Van Horne and Riley stress the importance of looking for clusters of "multiple cues to determine a person's intent."[75] Consider the above example; one anomaly is a man wearing sunglasses inside a grocery store. This should get our attention, but we need to look for more. Another anomaly is a man keeping his right hand hidden from view; most people "talk" with their hands to some extent. A third abnormal behavior for someone in a grocery store is looking at people, not groceries.

Condition Yellow doesn't come naturally. It's a learned behavior; you must learn to be aware of your surroundings and possible threats. This requires the study of

---

[75] (Van Horne & Riely, 2014)

people and their habits. In the police academy the most important safety measure that was driven into us was "Watch the hands." The hands are what hurt, the hands are what kill. A firearm left alone will not harm anyone. So, where do most people keep their hands? People in Condition White will usually keep their hands visible and engaged in their activity or conversation. Nearly 90% of people are right-handed, so almost everyone you watch will have their right hand visible and engaged. Once you are able to recognize "normal" it's easy to spot "abnormal." Abnormal should trigger a response. Most often the response is merely a heightened awareness.

> *"Watch the hands."*
> *The hands are what*
> *hurt you the hands are*
> *what kill.*

Van Horne and Riley make this observation:

> Studying body language accomplishes two objectives. The first is to identify those people who don't fit in and thus warrant further attention. The second is to predict people's behavior based on the subtle behavior cues that give away their intentions. These subtle and subconscious acts, rather than obvious movements, matter the most.[76]

This is Condition Yellow—being mentally in the game.

Condition Red

Condition Red is for engaging an enemy; it's the place to be when facing interpersonal human aggression.

---

[76] (Van Horne & Riely, 2014)

When an athlete moves from mental preparation to competitive playing he has transitioned to Condition Red. Grossman says that in Condition Red there are several physiological changes that take place. In Condition Red the heart rate jumps to 115-145 beats per minute (bpm) and fine motor skills deteriorate. The good news is complex motor skills, visual, and cognitive reaction time are at their peak. What does this mean? It means Condition Red is the "optimal survival and combat performance level."[77] Condition Red is where you *want* to be when engaged in a gunfight. Condition Red means a threat is imminent or an aggressor is shooting. If Condition Red is where we want to be in a gunfight, how do we get into and stay in Condition Red? Training and preparation. Condition Red is why reality based force-on-force scenario training is necessary. Training and preparation are why Stephen Curry can take critical fourth-quarter jump shots from beyond the 3-point line with a defender in his face and consistently make the shot. In Condition Red training and preparation take over and we operate on "automatic pilot." Automatic pilot and other phenomena associated with Condition Red is discussed in more detail in Chapter five.

What if we don't train and prepare? That's when Condition Black comes into play.

Condition Black

Condition Black is the place you don't want to be. In Condition Black the forebrain (the thinking part of the brain) shuts down. "As you enter into Condition Black, your cognitive processing deteriorates, which is a fancy way of saying that you stop thinking."[78] Hence, the response of one of the victims of the San Bernardino massacre, "I didn't

---

[77] (Grossman, On Combat, 2008, p. 30)
[78] (Grossman, On Combat, 2008, p. 44)

know what to do or say. I was just numb."[79] Increased heart rate enhances physical performance—to a point; after that tipping point, increased heart rate becomes counterproductive. Grossman says, "that even under the most ideal circumstances, above 175 bpm a catastrophic set of events begins to happen."[80]

> *"As you enter into Condition Black, your cognitive processing deteriorates, which is a fancy way of saying that you stop thinking."*
> —Dave Grossman

Grossman explains that the human brain is divided into three parts: the forebrain, midbrain, and hindbrain. Each part has a unique and distinctive function. The forebrain is where we do our thinking, unlike animals that have no forebrain. The forebrain is where we reason, consider, and decide. On the other hand, our midbrain doesn't think so much—it acts. The midbrain "performs extensive reflexive processes." The hindbrain is responsible for keeping our bodies alive and functioning by ensuring that things like the respiratory and cardiovascular systems are working.[81] When we enter Condition Black our midbrain and hindbrain literally take control and we are incapable of rational thought. We act and react based purely on survival instinct. This may sound reasonable, but when you are working not just for your own survival, but also for the survival of others you need every ounce of rational, logical thought.

In Condition Black your response may be to: (1) do nothing (fright response); (2) run (flight response); or (3) even engage the threat (fight response). But, whatever the response, it will be without thinking. It will be a reflexive response. While humans may have a predisposition to a survival mode, we can only respond out of what has been

---

[79] (Live interview of unidentified victim of the San Bernardino shooting, Fox News, December 3, 2015)
[80] (Grossman, On Combat, 2008, p. 43)
[81] (Grossman, On Combat, 2008, p. 43)

"stored" in our midbrain. Fear is a natural response. If someone walked into a grocery store,
church, or restaurant brandishing a
gun the natural response is fear. As
an armed protector, the idea is to
have a *controlled* response to fear. A
controlled response comes through
training and preparation.

> *A controlled re-*
> *sponse comes*
> *through training*
> *and preparation.*

    It's important to know these conditions aren't rungs
on a ladder, which naturally progress from one to the next.
Think of them as mental positions. Condition White is a
"sleeping position." While you may be wide awake, you are
mentally unaware of any potential threats and you might as
well be asleep. Condition White is fine while in a safe place
and you consciously go into Condition White. Condition
Yellow is a mental "sitting position." You are relaxed, in
conversation, listening to the preacher, or eating dinner with
a friend at a restaurant, but you remain aware of your surroundings. Condition Red is a "combat position." You are
taking positive action to eliminate a threat. The fight has be-
gun and you stay in the fight until the fight has ended and
the threat no longer exists. After the fight you will return to
Condition Yellow.

    Condition Black is unacceptable. Condition Black is
for the untrained and unprepared. Proper training and preparation will help avoid slipping into Condition Black. But
what if you do slip into Condition Black, is there any hope?
Yes, remember Condition Black is brought on by physiological changes that result in an increased heart rate. To get out
of it the heart rate must be reduced. Grossman says this can
be accomplished by intentional "tactical breathing." Basketball players lower their heart rate by taking slow deliberate
breathes just before shooting free-throws. Grossman recommends a four-count deep, slow, and deliberate sequence to
lower an elevated heart rate. He encourages people to try it
while reading through his breathing steps:

- In through the nose two, three, four. Hold two, three, four. Out through the lips two, three, four. Hold two, three, four.
- In through the nose deep, deep, deep. Hold two, three, four. Out through the lips deep, deep, deep. Hold two, three, four.
- In through the nose two, three, four. Hold two, three, four. Out through the lips two, three, four. Hold two, three, four.[82]

It is important to understand this is not meditative "Zen" type breathing. Kenneth Murray explains,

> [Grossman's tactical breathing] is a focused, on-purpose breathing drill that must be practiced and used regularly to have access to it at the Unconscious Competent [UC] level of cognition if it is to be the least bit useful. It will not be "remembered" during a life threatening event, hence it will not be accessible if not conditioned to the UC level. Very few people or organizations "get" this...it is a foot note. Yet it is one of the most important tools during a critical incident.[83]

The next chapter looks at how to get into and remain in Condition Red when the situation demands it.

---

[82] (Grossman, On Combat, 2008, p. 332)
[83] (Murray K. , 2016)

Real-Life Scenario Training

Chapter 7

Man with a knife

It was a busy, hot summer night on San Antonio's east side. I checked back into service after finishing a call, "41-01, I'm 10-8 [in service]." The dispatcher responded, "41-01 make ### Runnels Street, in the Sutton Homes for a disturbance, man holding his girlfriend at knifepoint. Use caution, no cover available." Because of the high volume of calls during the summer months it was common not have not to have a cover or back-up officer available. I acknowledged and responded, "10-4, 41-01, I'm on the way." I arrived and found EMS technicians outside the first floor apartment. One of the technicians was peeking into the apartment through a window, "I think she may have the knife," he said.

Hoping the situation was defused and with my right hand on my holstered service revolver, I rapped loudly on the outer screen door with my left hand. "Police, open the door!" I commanded. The interior steel door slowly swung inward and standing not three feet away, with only a screen door between us, was a rather large woman standing behind a much shorter man. The woman's arms were tightly wrapped around the short man's body. They struggled for control of a seven-inch butcher knife and yelled at each other in Spanish. Drawing my revolver I pointed it at the man's head and demanded "Drop the knife!" I repeated over and over while pushing on the screen door, with my left hand in a fruitless attempt to open it. "Drop the knife, or I'll shoot!" The man refused. Unable to open the screen door I started to squeeze the trigger. I could see the hammer of the .357 magnum coming back...the knife dropped. Relaxing my finger I allowed the hammer to come to rest without discharging the gun. I holstered the revolver—"Whew, that was a close one," I thought. It was then I noticed the screen door opened out by pulling it; all the while I was trying to push on it. The man was arrested without further incident.

Why didn't I notice the screen door opened out in the heat of battle? Because my mind was focused on the immediate threat, the knife. Fear-induced stress decreases one's ability to think through all aspects of a situation. With all my focus on the knife and the protection of the victim my mind wouldn't allow my eyes to leave the threat and look at the screen door to determine why it wouldn't open.

How should we prepare if we know that in a fear-induced event (e.g. a gunfight) both fine motor skills and reasoning skills will be affected? By using fear-induced, force-on-force, real-life scenario training.

Obviously real guns, knives, and ammunition can't be used in scenario based training, but something that comes close needs to be used. The question is, how can an instructor mimic the physiological and psychological changes that are induced by fear in a training environment? Grossman advises, "[W]arriors can (and must) be inoculated against this [fear-induced] stressor by experiencing force-on-force scenarios in which they shoot and are shot at by paint-filled, gunpowder propelled, plastic bullets."[84]

---

[84] (Grossman, On Combat, 2008, p. 38)

Fear-induced, force-on-force, real-life scenario training

Fear-induced, force-on-force, real-life scenario training is critical to train our bodies to enter into Condition Red, while avoiding Condition Black. As discussed in the previous chapter, Condition Red is the optimal fighting level. At this level there are physiological changes that take place, one is an elevated the heart rate. Basketball players get elevated heart rates when they run up and down the court. In order to perform under these physically demanding conditions players train and prepare by physically exerting themselves. However, as we have seen with Stephen Curry, there's also a mental element to the game. Curry prepares mentally for specific situations that he anticipates by visualizing the situation and practicing the shot. You too must prepare in like manner for a gun battle, where the stakes are much higher.

After research revealed heart rate is significantly elevated during a gunfight police trainers responded. In an attempt to simulate real-life conditions police firearms instructors began having students physically exert themselves by doing exercises to elevate their heart rates before engaging the target. I remember attending early police in-service training in which we repeated shooting the qualification course-of-fire, but with exercises before each stage. The instructor would give the command, "Run-in-place until you hear the whistle, at which time you will stop, draw your service pistol and shoot three rounds. Ready, begin." As you would expect, the scores dropped considerably.

At the time this was advanced cutting-edge firearms training. It demonstrated how much harder it was to accurately shoot when out of breath (trying to maintain a proper sight picture when sucking for air is difficult for the best of shooters). But further research demonstrated there is a difference between an elevated heart rate brought on by physical exertion and one caused by fear. Grossman points out that physical exertion causes the blood vessels to open up, pumping extra blood to the muscles and providing much needed oxygen. The increased flow of blood throughout the body normally causes a person's face to turn beet red or become flush with color. However, a "fear-induced" elevated heart rate will usually cause the face to turn white or to lose color.[85] Hence the expression, "He turned white as a sheet."

There's a reason for this phenomenon. It's called "vasoconstriction." Rather than opening up (as during physical exertion), the blood vessels constrict, limiting blood flow. Grossman explains,

> We are not sure why this happens, but the current, dominate theory is that the physical demands cause the body to scream for oxygen while the vasoconstriction shuts down the blood flow that provides oxygen, causing the heart to beat ever faster while achieving very little.[86]

So what's the effect of vasoconstriction? A loss of fine motor skills. The phenomenon of vasoconstriction is experienced in the cold. When your body starts to get cold it automatically responds by restricting blood flow to non-vital extremities. God designed the body to understand that fingers and toes can become cold and even frozen, yet the body can survive—fingers and toes aren't needed to live. That's why our hands and feet get cold so easily. The result is a loss of dexterity. Fine motor skills are out the window. If you've ever tried to write down something while your hands are cold then you've experienced this loss of dexterity. Depending on how cold your hands are will make the task range from difficult to impossible. What's the take away? Fear-induced

---

[85] (Grossman, On Combat, 2008, p. 44)
[86] (Grossman, On Combat, 2008, p. 44)

stress causes the loss of fine motor skills and decreases your ability to think through situations.

There are a number of tools police use for force-on-force training. These include paintball guns, airsoft guns, non-lethal paint marking ammunition, and laser guns. The Reality Based Training industry is constantly improving training and coming up with training devices to better mimic real-life situations. The best and latest technology is very expensive, but for relatively low cost a high level of training can be conducted. It's critical to accept scenario training as serious training; this isn't paintball gaming or laser tag. The purpose for using projectiles is to increase arousal by the threat of pain. Pain-induced fear best mimics the fear brought on by interpersonal human aggression.

Kenneth Murray has written an exceptional book on putting together real-life scenario based training entitled *Training at the Speed of Life, Vol. 1*. I would be foolish to attempt to duplicate his work.

In the Heat of Battle: Condition Red

In chapter six I presented the four levels of awareness. Grossman uses the colors white, yellow, red, and black to describe these levels of awareness. Condition Red is the "optimal survival and combat performance level."[87] Condition Red is where you *want* to be when engaged in a gunfight. However, getting into and staying in Condition Red takes training and preparation to overcome obstacles that prevent or hinder one's optimal awareness level. One obstacle affects almost every single person. There is an innate fear in nearly every human being. It's the fear of interpersonal human aggression.

---

[87] (Grossman, On Combat, 2008, p. 30)

Grossman calls the fear of interpersonal human aggression the "Universal Human Phobia."[88] A phobia is more than rational fear. The Farlex Partner Medical Dictionary defines phobia as "any objectively unfounded morbid dread or fear that arouses a state of panic."[89] A person in a state of panic isn't thinking straight, or isn't thinking at all. Responding to fear is one thing, having a phobic-scale response is another. Grossman uses the following example. If a person walked into a crowded room with a pistol and started shooting someone in the room, "up to 98 percent of the average audience [the others in the room] would experience a true phobic-scale response."[90] In other words, 98 percent of the people in the room would have a response that is irrational. Someone must have a *rational* response to stop the person from shooting others. It's not time to talk, to negotiate, or even to pray—it's time to act and to react effectively. To stop the killing someone must respond rationally. Police Lt. Como comments,

> Many a martial artist and marksman has found out, to their dismay, that merely practicing a technique or drill over and over again, while ignoring the psychological aspects of combat, most often had the opposite result of what the intense training was meant to instill.[91]

A trained, prepared, and properly equipped protector in the above example would have been in Condition Yellow and at the sight of the pistol immediately moved to Condition Red. Then he or she would have taken action—quick action—to stop the aggressor. The protector needs to have a

---

[88] (Grossman, On Combat, 2008, pp. 2-7)
[89] (Farlex Partner Medical Dictionary, 2012)
[90] (Grossman, On Combat, 2008, p. 3)
[91] (Como as quoted by Murray, 2006, p. 20)

> *The protector needs to have a plan in place* before *an incident occurs so the response is both reflective and automatic.*

plan in place *before* an incident occurs so the response is both reflective and automatic.

It is necessary to take immediate and appropriate action in a gunfight. In order to do so, one must be *able* to take action. As discussed in chapter five, there are physiological changes the body experiences in the heat of battle for which we must be prepared (i.e. increased heart rate, vasoconstriction, and loss of fine motor skills). Like athletes that prepare to perform at the highest level when the game is on the line, those armed to protect others also need to prepare to perform. Training and preparation are necessary to get in a fighting mindset (Condition Red) and stay there for the duration of a gunfight.

Conclusion

One critical form of preparation is Reality Based Training. The idea is to transition from Condition Yellow to Condition Red, the optimal "fighting zone" smoothly and quickly. In Condition Red your heart rate increases, enabling you to react more effectively with a heighted sense of awareness. However, there's a tipping point. At some point the heart rate increases too much, usually in excess of 175 beats per minute.[92] A sensory overload causes excessive heart rate and the effects of the increased heart rate turns negative and you slip into Condition Black. The idea is to respond from Condition Red when your body is at its peak—when you are in "a fighting mindset."

---

[92] (Grossman, On Combat, 2008, p. 43)

93

Part Three

The Body

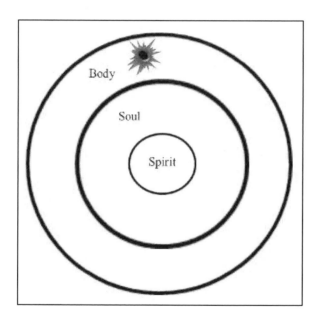

Firearm Basics

Chapter 8

My first fast draw

In the early 1980s, retention duty-holsters (so named because of their design to prevent someone from snatching an officer's gun from the holster) were just becoming popular. One of the "lessons" prisoners were learning behind bars was to take a police officer's gun away and use it on the officer. This put the manufacturers of police duty-holsters in a dilemma. They could manufacture a holster for a "quick draw" and could manufacture a holster for ultimate security. But could one holster do both? The goal of a retention duty-holster is to allow the handgun to be drawn safely and quickly by the officer while making it difficult for someone else to remove the gun from the holster. In order to achieve this goal, retention holsters have special buttons, snaps, straps, bands, and a slew of other specially engineered release devices.

In 1983 the San Antonio Police Department issued the duty revolver, but cadets were responsible to purchase their own holsters. I opted for one of the new retention holsters manufactured by Safariland®. During the police academy I trained and practiced drawing from the holster and continued to practice after graduation. But in the back of my mind was an ever-present nagging question, "Would I be able to draw my revolver quickly and smoothly at the moment of truth?"

One Sunday afternoon, shortly after graduation from the police academy, I was assigned to district 1-1 patrolling the downtown area. It was a slow and peaceful afternoon; the police radio was silent and there was little traffic as I drove past a white male walking alone. Walking the same direction I was driving, I could see he had his left hand in the front pocket of his gray hoody, and his right hand swinging naturally at his side. As I drove past he glanced at me with a nervous look. I noticed a curved metal band that looked like the back strap of a revolver in the hoody pocket. Making four right turns I came up behind him again and notified the dispatcher, "1-1, I'll be out at Lexington and St. Mary's with a white male, who possibly has a gun." "Ten-four, 1-1," the dispatcher responded.

After pulling up behind the suspect, I stopped and put my patrol cruiser in park. I opened the driver's door, took a position behind the door, and as I was yelling for the suspect to stop I noticed my revolver was already in my hand pointed at the threat. Without thinking I had drawn my revolver quickly and smoothly at the moment of truth. The suspect complied with my commands and I discovered that the metal band I thought might be a handgun was actually part of a Walkman® radio he had just stolen.

After that incident, I never again had that nagging concern about not being able to draw my service handgun quickly and smoothly when necessary. Training and preparation had paid off.

The early 80s also saw a large shift in police firearms training. By 1983 police were taking significant strides to move from marksmanship training to combat pistol training. Fourteen years earlier, in 1968 when California Highway (CHP) Patrol Trooper Gore was a cadet, the CHP academy focused on marksmanship. Marksmanship teaches the basics of how to safely and accurately shoot at a paper target. Cadet

Gore was good; in fact Gore finished at the top of his class.[93] The other three officers killed in the Newhall shooting were also accomplished marksmen. Then why were two ex-convicts able to out shoot and gun down four troopers? Because a gunfight is different from target shooting.

The two assailants had trained themselves to fight with guns. As has been demonstrated earlier, and as anyone who has been in an actual gunfight will attest to, shooting at a human being that's trying to kill you is far different from shooting at a paper target in a controlled environment. Mike Hall saw firearms training as a key reason for the Newhall massacre. At the time the CHP taught cadets marksmanship, but they didn't teach handgun combat skills, "The only trouble is that the CHP's program was oriented toward teaching marksmanship, while what Cadet Gore really needed was training in how to fight with firearms, a different matter entirely."[94]

This is offense, not defense. When the bad guy comes— Condition Red.

A gunfight is just that, a fight with guns. Longtime war correspondent John Steinbeck observed, "This is the law: The purpose of fighting is to win. There is no possible victory in defense. The sword is more important than the shield, and skill is more important than either. The final weapon is the brain. All else is supplemental."[95] Firearms expert Massad Ayoob agrees, his third priority of survival is "Skill with Safety Equipment".[96]

> "The purpose of fighting is to win. There is no possible victory in defense."
> —John Steinbeck

---

[93] (Wood, 2013, p. 156)
[94] (Wood, 2013, p. 157)
[95] (Murray K. R., 2004, p. 14)
[96] (Wood, 2013, p. 124)

One must be familiar with and able to use his or her equipment. This means you need to be competent and proficient with your handgun. Marksmanship proficiency is necessary, but marksmanship is only the first step. You must learn how to fight with a gun. You must be able to demonstrate the skill necessary to not only shoot accurately, but to properly and effectively use your handgun in a gunfight.

Cardinal rules

Every training session, whether it's classroom instruction, Reality Based Training (using non-lethal guns), or actual live-fire training should begin with a review of the four cardinal rules of gun safety developed by Colonel Jeff Cooper:

1. Treat every gun as if it is loaded.
2. Never point the muzzle at anything you are not willing to destroy.
3. Keep your finger off the trigger and out of the trigger guard until you are on target and ready to shoot.
4. Be aware of your target and beyond.

Rule number one, *"Treat every gun as if it is loaded,"* is violated on a regular basis. Far too often I've witnessed a person hand a gun to someone else and say, "Don't worry, it's not loaded." In my firearms training classes my son and I teach that it is the responsibility of both the person handing off the gun and the person receiving the gun to ensure the gun is unloaded. It's not uncommon to hear media reports of someone being shot by a person who thought a gun was unloaded.

Treating every gun as if it is loaded means you should never violate rule number two, *"Never point the muzzle at anything you are not willing to destroy."* That seems so simple. Don't point a gun at other people, pets, TVs, couches, lamps, etc. Keep in mind, this rule also includes being careful not to inadvertently point a gun at yourself (including fingers, hands, or feet). If practicing dry-firing (dry-firing is detailed below) then ensure the gun is pointed in a safe direction at something that will stop a bullet.

Rule number three, *"Keep your finger off the trigger and out of the trigger guard until you are on target and ready to shoot,"* is the most common violation of the rules seen on the gun range. It's been my experience that the violation of this rule is the primary cause of unintentional discharges on the gun range. Shooters should learn to properly grip a handgun by running their trigger finger along the side of the gun (outside the trigger guard), pointed in the same direction as the muzzle. There's no need to insert a finger inside the trigger guard and on the trigger until on target and ready to shoot. Keeping the trigger finger off the trigger and outside the trigger guard (along the side of the frame) will help prevent an unintentional discharge caused from a sympathetic response. A sympathetic response is an instinctive "knee jerk" reaction.  Think about how fingers instinctively contract when a person suddenly reaches to catch an object. All four fingers and the thumb respond reflexively. The same thing happens when a person is startled—the fingers suddenly contract. What happens when a finger is on the trigger and the person is startled? *Bang!*

The fourth cardinal rule, *"Be aware of your target and beyond,"* is a common violation that occurs away from a controlled gun range. Most gun ranges have solid backstops designed to stop bullet travel and lessen the chance of ricochets. However, hunters and shooters (at a place other than a gun range), often violate this rule even when they think they're not. You must always consider where the bullet will travel to after it passes through the target, or if the target is missed. The bullet must be stopped—something or someone will stop it.

These four rules should be committed to memory and put into practice by everyone who handles any type of firearm.

Basic Marksmanship

Retired Border Patrol Assistant Chief Patrol Inspector, combat pistol instructor, and author Bill Jordan wrote:

> The only dependable way to learn to shoot a handgun is to start with deliberate, aimed, single action fire at a bull's-eye target until the fundamentals of trigger squeeze and sight alignment are thoroughly mastered. Only then should the shooter concern himself with fast double action shooting.[97]

Basic marksmanship skills should be demonstrated prior to combat pistol or tactical pistol training. Basic shooting fundamentals are:

1. *Stance.* Stance is the platform for shooting. A shaky platform results in a shaky shot. In marksmanship shooting there are traditionally two stances: the Weaver (standing bladed to the target, a right handed shooter shooting to the left) and the Isosceles (standing square to the target, the target directly in front of the shooter). For combat shooting the optimal stance is a modification of either of

---

[97] (Jordan, 1965, p. 91)

these by incorporating an athletic stance. Think of a boxer—feet shoulder width apart, knees bent, shoulders over the toes, and weight forward. One that lends itself to stability.

2. *Grip.* The grip should be a natural pointing grip. Thumbs along the side of the gun opposite the trigger finger, pointing  down range. The grip should be firm, but not a white-knuckled-death grip. Don't attempt to completely stop the gun from moving.  Anyone who has a heartbeat and is breathing will cause the gun to move.

3. *Sight alignment.* Sight alignment is the 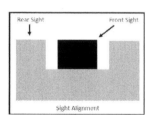 alignment of the front sight (sight at the muzzle) and rear sight (sight above grips). The sights should be even across the top with even space on either side of the front sight.

4. *Sight picture.* The sight picture includes the sight alignment and the point of aim

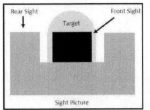

on the target. The human eye can only focus at one distance at a time. It's impossible to focus on the rear sight, front sight, and the target at the same time. Focus on the front sight and use your peripheral vision to align the rear sight and target to the front sight; both the rear sight and the target will be out of focus. This may seem unnatural at first, since shooters are tempted to focus on the target. However, you must keep the focus on the front sight. Remember the gun will still move slightly, and the front sight may seem to "dance" a little.

5. *Trigger control.* To help control the trigger, trigger "slack" or "play" needs to be taken up. After the slack is taken out of the trigger the trigger should be pressed straight to the rear, evenly and smoothly. Shooters shouldn't attempt to anticipate when the hammer will fall (or the sear disengages) and the gun discharges.

6. *Breathing.* Shooters should breathe normally, and then "cut-off" breathing when the trigger slack is taken up—just before the first shot is fired. You can shoot as many rounds as you are comfortable with before taking another breath.

7. *Follow through.* Follow through is maintaining a firm grip while allowing the gun to recoil and then coming back to position. Don't fight it, go with it.

Fundamental shooting skills can be learned in a rather short amount of time. Any competent firearms instructor should be able to safely and effectively teach almost anyone how to safely and accurately shoot a handgun. However, to maintain and increase fundamental shooting skills regular training and practice are necessary. One easy and inexpensive form of practice is *dry-firing*. Dry-firing is conducted with an **unloaded** gun in a safe place. Dry-firing is the exercise of practicing stance, grip, sight alignment, sight picture, trigger control, and breathing without shooting live ammunition. Follow through may even be simulated. Start by unloading the gun—double and triple check it to be absolutely sure. Once the gun is unloaded remove any live ammunition from the room in which the dry-fire practice will take place. After following these safety measures you are ready to begin training. The vast majority of modern handguns will not be damaged by dry-firing them. You can check with your gun manufacturer to confirm the safety of dry firing your particular handgun.

During dry-firing practice a "target" that will stop a real bullet should always be used. Even after all the safety measures, one cartridge may be missed (remember rule #2). In order to dry-fire a semi-automatic pistol the slide will need to be racked each time the trigger is pulled to reset the trigger. The purpose of dry-firing is muscle memory. Dry-firing should be done slowly and methodically. Every step should be thought through: stance, grip, sight alignment, sight picture, and breathing control. When everything is right, front sight is in focus—sharp and crisp, trigger slack is taken up, breathing "cut-off", then the trigger is slowly pressed rearward until the hammer falls (or sear is released). When the gun goes "click" the trigger should be held back. If using a revolver slowly release pressure on the trigger allowing it to go forward until it resets, repeat the dry-fire exercise. If using a semi-automatic, while continuing to hold the trigger back, rack the slide, get back on target and slowly release the trigger allowing it to go forward until it resets. Repeat the dry-fire exercise.

As you become more proficient going through the motions of proper marksmanship the speed of the exercise should increase a little at a time. Proper training and form produces good muscle memory habits. When the moment of truth comes the muscles will instinctively respond rightly. To those unfamiliar with marksmanship, dry-firing may seem silly, but I know of no accomplished shooter that doesn't practice dry-firing. In fact, there are now training guns available exclusively for dry-firing. These training aids allow shooters to practice safely and without needing to rack the slide to reset the trigger.

Live-fire training

When I was a police officer, the department required annual firearms qualification. Each year every officer attended a week of "In-Service" training at the police academy. One day, or at least half of a day, was dedicated to firearms qualification. (That most states require their police officers to qualify only annually comes as a surprise to many.) The normal procedure for "range day" was to begin with classroom instruction, reviewing shooting fundamentals. After being reminded about trigger control, sight alignment, sight picture, grip, stance, breathing, and so forth the officers headed out to the range. The range master would explain the course-of-fire and officers shot a practice course-of-fire to "warm-up". This gave the firearms instructors the opportunity to correct problems shooters were experiencing. Following the practice course-of-fire a qualifying round would be shot. The vast majority of officers qualified with an 85% or better. A 70% was required for qualification. The problem is real-life doesn't work that way. When an officer gets called to a disturbance no one stops them and says, "Hold on, at this call you'll be involved in a shooting. Let's go over the fundamentals of shooting and warm up with a few practice shots before you make the call." In the mid-1990s, when I was assigned as the sergeant in charge of firearms training we decided to change things. When officers showed up for range day we had the class go immediately to the range, with no classroom instruction. When told the first course-of-fire was for qualification we heard the moans and complaints, "That's not fair, we need some warm-up shots." Needless to say the scores went down, but the firearms instructors had a better idea of the officers' skill—and so did the officers.

Former Central Intelligence Agency (CIA) officer and author of *The Covert Guide to Concealed Carry*, Jason Hanson, recommends the Federal Bureau of Investigation (FBI) course adopted in January 2013. Hanson writes,

> Every government agency likes to think they're the best. So whether or not you're a fan of the FBI, there is one thing the Bureau is good at... and that's keeping statistics on shootings. Over the years, the FBI has documented and studied thousands of shootings, and in January of this year the FBI changed its qualification course based on the feedback of these shootings. In short, the old course involved shooting at far distances as much as 50 yards, but the new course focuses on close

quarters shooting since the majority of gun-fights occur at seven yards or less.[98]

See appendix "A" for the FBI's course of fire.

In his book, *Training at the Speed of Life, Vol. 1,* Kenneth Murray writes about a one-shot qualification advocated by former Orlando Police Department range master, O. Frank Repass:

> Repass has extensive research and experience demonstrating that if you can hit a five inch by ten inch target that is hanging at a bladed angle, from a "ready gun" position at five yards in less than 1.5 seconds, you have mastered the use of your handgun to the level necessary for delivering swift and accurate fire under realistic conditions. After you have "qualified," the rest of the time spent at the range can be dedicated to learning how to fight with your pistol.[99]

Murray argues this moves firearms training from the traditional "*qualification* paradigm toward a competency-based demonstration of proficiency."[100] As of this writing, Repass' one-shot qualification hasn't been widely adopted by law enforcement. However, it should not be dismissed out of hand. Repass' one-shot qualification is a great marker of where someone is at in their proficiency with a handgun. The distance (five yards), the target (5"x10"), and the time (1.5 seconds) all provide a realistic and achievable goal.

For years there has been a trend by law enforcement firearms trainers to move away from numeric scores to a "pass" or "fail" score. Firearms records of officers involved

---

[98] (Hanson, 2013)
[99] (Murray K. R., 2004, p. 25)
[100] (Murray K. R., 2004, p. 25)

in shootings are routinely subpoenaed as evidence. Defense attorneys use scores to cast doubt in the minds of jurors as to officers' intentions and justification for using lethal force. If an officer is an outstanding marksman with high shooting scores, an unscrupulous attorney may question why more than half of the officer's shots missed in an attempt to show the officer was unsure of his or her decision to shoot. Although we know from research traditional marksmanship doesn't equal being in a real gunfight, jurors don't know that. On the other hand, if an officer scored the minimum (i.e. 70%) an attorney may attempt to question the officer's qualification to even be in law enforcement. By having a pass/fail scoring system all of a department's records are the same: passing. Those failing are disqualified from carrying a firearm until they pass.

While numeric scores have value in showing improvement in marksmanship, remember basic marksmanship is just the foundation for combat or tactical shooting.

Live-fire shooting positions

Live-fire training should involve shooting from these three positions: the low-ready, drawing from the holster, and the safety circle. Of paramount concern is muzzle awareness. *While handling any firearm always be attentive to where the muzzle of the gun is pointed!*

Low-ready

A beginning shooter should first learn to shoot from the "low-ready" standing position. In the low-ready position the shooter is standing in their shooting stance, facing the target, holding the handgun with the proper grip, the hands lowered down to about a 45-degree angle from the body. At the command to fire the shooter simply raises their arms bringing the gun up to obtain a proper sight picture. After firing the shooter returns to the low-ready position.

Drawing from holster

After fundamental skills are learned, training to draw from a holster is the natural next step. Holster training should be practiced with an unloaded gun (or better, an inert training gun of the same model as the real gun) until a level of confidence and competence is reached. Start slow! As demonstrated in the above story of my first fast draw, speed will be the natural result of proper training.

Basic geometry teaches that the shortest distance between two points is a straight line. A straight line from the holster to the sight picture is the fastest and safest draw. Begin from the shooting stance with a proper grip on the holstered gun. See chapter ten for a better understanding of selecting a holster and ensuring a proper grip while your gun is seated in it. Slowly remove the gun from the holster while your finger remains outside of the trigger guard. At the same time bring your support hand over to your drawing hand to complete a correct two-handed grip as the gun is "punched" into a proper sight picture. Practice this several times until it comes naturally. You should be able to grip, draw, and get a sight picture without taking your eyes off the target.

Once a level of comfort is reached going from the grip to the draw, and then to the sight picture, it's time to move to the next level. Instead of beginning from a shooting stance move to making the draw from a more realistic one. For instance, start from a natural position like talking with someone in a normal conversation. Your hands should be relaxed at your side. From there you want to transition to the shooting stance, draw, and obtain your sight picture. Again, start slowly and methodically. When drawing and getting on target from a natural posture becomes comfortable put on a jacket, vest, or shirt to conceal the gun, as it would normally be carried. With clothing covering the gun, you will need to learn to push or pull the clothing out of the way before obtaining a grip on the gun. Neglecting to practice with the gun concealed by clothing may cause you to grab a handful of clothing along with the gun at the moment of truth. Next practice drawing from a variety of other positions you may face (i.e. sitting, kneeling, or crouching).

Just a few minutes of daily practice will produce dramatic results. After becoming competent off the range, practice drawing from the holster during live-fire training.

Safety Circle

In addition to learning the low-ready position and drawing from the holster, the "safety circle" is a third critical position to learn. The safety circle allows for safely moving with a loaded gun out of the holster and ready for quick use. In the safety circle, the handgun is held close to the front of

Safety Circle

the body with the muzzle pointed straight down. To obtain the safety circle place the support hand just below the chest but above the stomach with the palm facing your body, elbow straight out, and thumb up. Using a proper grip on the gun in the primary shooting hand and muzzle pointed down, place the gun on top of the support hand with thumbs pressed against each other. From this position you are able to punch the gun straight out into a shooting position. This position is used for moving tactically either

111

alone or with a team. It's called the safety circle because the gun is pointed down, in a safe direction, allowing someone to move in any direction without unintentionally pointing the muzzle at something they are unwilling to destroy (see Rule #2).

In bygone times, the low-ready was the position of choice when moving, but the safety circle is safer for both individual and team movement. With practice the safety circle will become second nature.

Although these three basic positions should be mastered, you should also practice shooting from a variety of positions. The one constant in a gunfight is the inconsistency of your surroundings or circumstances. Advanced tactical training should include shooting from other positions such as kneeling, crouching, sitting, prone, back, etc.

Cover/Concealment

Cover and *concealment* are two terms that are sometimes confusing and erroneously used interchangeably. *Cover* is any object you are able to place between yourself and the aggressor that will stop bullets. The thick bullet-proof glass in a bank drive-through is cover, although its transparency doesn't provide concealment. *Concealment* is any object that conceals you from the aggressor's vision— either completely or partially. Concealment may or may not be cover. Concealment can be a cardboard box, a wall, curtains, or a door. Concealment may even be darkness.

Interior house walls provide concealment, but not cover. Virtually all handgun calibers, including .22 caliber, will easily pass through two sheets of drywall. Furthermore, most will also travel through one or two 2x4 studs. Bullets will also easily pass through common interior doors and most exterior doors.

Part of situational awareness is recognizing what cover and/or concealment is available at any given time.

Cover is better than concealment—concealment is better than nothing. It is good to recognize that even if concealment

> Cover is better than concealment—con-cealment is better than nothing.

cannot stop bullets many people are either unaware that bullets will pass through most objects (such as doors, chairs, walls, etc.) and/or they will instinctively attempt to shoot around concealment. Therefore, use cover if available, but don't underestimate the use of concealment if cover isn't available. Also, the aggressor may be using concealment you can shoot through, but be sure of what is beyond the target. If the aggressor is behind a wall, who else is on the other side? If the aggressor is peeking over the top of a chair or around a sheetrock wall to present a smaller target, recognize that a bullet can penetrate the chair or wall, offering a larger target to shoot.

Never hesitate to use cover or concealment, no matter how small or flimsy it is. At the San Antonio police academy cadets were put through a concealment scenario during police tactics training. Cadets were given the following scenario: "You have been pursuing a man wanted for murder and who has already shot your partner. He is armed with a gun and swears he won't be taken alive. During the foot pursuit you chase him into a room where you confront him. He's the only one in the room. There is no one else." With that information each cadet was sent into the room. As the cadet entered the room the cadet found the bad guy hiding behind a long piece of cardboard held in one hand. With his other hand he was attempting to point his gun at the cadet from around the side of the cardboard. Many cadets attempted to maneuver around the cardboard to get a "clear" shot rather than simply shooting through the cardboard. The point of the exercise was to get the cadet to think about cover and concealment. Under the stress of the scenario many didn't think, "That's simply cardboard, I can shoot right through it."

The scenario aims to teach two important things: for the cadet (1) to know and be aware of the capabilities of the service ammunition; and (2) to understand the psychological advantage of using concealment. Just as the "bad guy" in the scenario used concealment to his advantage, so too should police officers. Cover is best—use when available; concealment is better than nothing.

Movement

"Action always beats reaction," the police academy instructor told our class. Unfortunately, the protector of innocent lives on American soil is, more often than not, reacting to an action and is therefore disadvantaged in a gunfight. Hence, the protector needs to gain any possible advantage—that advantage may be movement.

In the absence of cover or concealment, use movement. In the Newhall shooting (detailed in chapter four) the ex-convicts were constantly moving and shooting. All four officers that were gunned down took up static positions from which to shoot. The bad guys gained the advantage of shooting at stationary targets while the officers were shooting at moving targets. But in order to shoot on the move you must train using movement. As with any firearms training, begin with an unloaded or inert training gun.

Recall that in the Newhall shooting there was one other "good guy" who was involved in the shooting. Mr. Gary Kness, a former Marine, happened to be driving by at the time of the shooting. Initially, Mr. Kness thought a movie was being filmed when he saw the two police cruisers and the red Pontiac in the parking lot. He decided to act after realizing he was witnessing a real police shooting, Mr. Kness bailed out of his car and ran to where Officer Allyen was lying wounded. Mr. Kness grabbed the officer's shotgun from the ground and tried to fire it, but found it empty. After attempting to drag the downed officer out of the line of fire

114

he picked up Allyen's revolver and shot one time at Davis, hitting him in the arm. The next time Mr. Kness pulled the trigger it fell on a spent casing. Mr. Kness fled from the danger zone into a ditch when he heard the sirens of the responding patrols. He knew he might be mistaken for one of the criminals before he could safely make himself known to other officers.

In his analysis of the shooting, Mike Wood comments, "There are certainly many reasons why Mr. Kness avoided injury, but the fact that he was continuously moving while on the battlefield was certainly preeminent among them and constitutes a powerful lesson for today's warriors."[101] Moving and shooting is very dangerous and should only be attempted after receiving training and supervision from a qualified firearms instructor. However, because moving provides such an excellent advantage it behooves anyone carrying a firearm for personal protection to receive the necessary instruction and practice with it regularly.

> *Because moving provides such an excellent advantage it behooves anyone carrying a firearm for personal protection to receive the necessary instruction and practice with it regularly.*

Tactical or combat shooting is more than just standing and shooting at paper targets. It includes decision making, addressing multiple targets, moving and shooting, reloading, clearing malfunctions, and other types of shooting that better mimics a gunfight.

Combat training needs to include shooting from very close quarters—from arm's length out to 15 yards. This is shooting without using the gun sights. The fact is, in a gunfight you will be focused on the threat, not your front sight. Survival instincts take over and just like Reality Based

---

[101] (Wood, 2013, p. 153)

Training, combat shooting aims to give you an instinctual response in the moment of truth.

Combat Shooting: An old way to shoot revived

Chapter 9

A Long Journey

At the age most kids enter college, trade school, or start their first fulltime job, I entered the world of "police" firearms training. That was 1979, the summer after I graduated from high school. As a young airman in the Security Police Academy at Lackland Air Force Base in San Antonio, Texas I was introduced to formal combat firearms training. Air Force security police officers were required to qualify with: Smith and Wesson's model 15 .38 caliber revolver; Winchester's model 1200 .12-gauge shotgun; and Colt's M-16, 5.56 (.223) caliber fully automatic rifle. The firearms training consisted of learning the nomenclature of our weapons, how to clean them, and proper marksmanship shooting from the standing, kneeling, and prone positions. In order to make it "combat" shooting the basic shooting positions were combined with shooting from the left-side, right-side, and over barricade positions.

I wasn't all that confident in my ability to successfully fight with a handgun even after qualifying as an expert marksman and earning the ribbons as a testament to it. As I recall, all handgun shooting was from 7 to 25 yards. Following my discharge in 1983, I joined the San Antonio Police Department (SAPD). In the police academy I tied another cadet for top shooter in class 83B. Firearms training included using both an indoor and an outdoor range and focused on marksmanship shooting. At the time, the police academy's firearm's training was much like the marksmanship shooting of the Air Force.

In an effort to reinforce marksmanship, our department participated in the National Rifle Association's (NRA) police marksmanship program. Officers qualifying as sharpshooter, expert, or distinguished marksman earned badges that could be proudly displayed on their uniform. Badges were earned by point scoring on a silhouette target. The closer the hit was to the center of the target, the higher the score. Shooting a "tight group" was sought and rewarded. A tight group means grouping your shots as close to each other as possible. The NRA badge, like the ribbon awarded by the Air Force, amply described the type of shooting: *marksmanship*.

In 1987 I attended an NRA Law Enforcement Firearms Instructor's Course. After the forty-hour course I was certified to teach police officers the fine art of shooting. And that's exactly what it was—a *fine art*. The NRA course emphasized the importance of firearms safety and shooting fundamentals. To consistently shoot tight groups the fundamentals of marksmanship training is critical. That's all well and good when distance and time permit. But the fact of the matter is, in a real gunfight distance and time are two things you rarely have control over. Far more often than not, it's the assailant that dictates distance and time.

> *In a real gunfight distance and time are two things you rarely have control over.*

Distance and *time*, coupled with the fact that police tactics had evolved into training with nonlethal projectile-

118

shooting training aids, got me thinking more about something I had heard of called "point shooting" or "instinctive shooting." Also, my age started to affect my eyesight. At first only my very close vision was impaired. I could still clearly see and focus on the front sight of my handgun at arm's length. Hence, I was still able to consistently hit the target, and produce the all-important "tight group" that shooters revere. But over time my near-sightedness became worse, and soon even at arm's length my sights were blurry. Was "point" or "instinctive" shooting the answer?

While thinking about instinctive shooting and not being able to focus on my front sight, I dusted off my copy of Bill Jordan's *No Second Place Winner*. Jordan advocates not using your sights for combat or point shooting. He suggests using what he calls "hip shooting" at distances from 0-3 yards. Jordan writes,

> [T]he shot can be fired at utmost speed and a hit made on a reasonable sized target without the necessity of stopping the gun and consciously bringing it into alignment. The shot can be fired as part of the draw— as soon as the gun clears the holster and is rocked into line. At such close ranges "aiming" is solely by feel.[102]

Are you kidding me? *Shooting without looking at your sights?* This has always been one of the BIG "No, Nos" in the world of police training. One of the biggest objections to teaching officers not to use their sights is liability. Unfortunately, in the world of policing many poor decisions are made based on

Are you kidding me? Shooting without looking at your sights?

---

[102] (Jordan, 1965, pp. 91-92)

the fear of being sued. Lawsuits are doubled edged swords. On one hand, lawsuits have provided the incentive needed for government entities to provide improved police training. On the other hand, lawsuits (or the fear of them) have hampered commonsense training. Not only does Jordan advocate ditching the sights, he doesn't seem to care about a tight group! He simply says a hit can be made "on a reasonable sized target."

For years I was told, trained, and trained others that the most important thing to remember for shooting accurately was focusing on the front sight. Do you want a tight group? Then have a proper stance, grip, sight alignment, sight picture, trigger control, breathing, and follow through—and most importantly *focus on the front sight!* Do these things, and you'll have a tight group. But is a tight group the goal? If it is, we're achieving that goal. But if the goal is to win gunfights, most of which take place at close quarters in just seconds, we're not preparing and training properly to achieve that goal.

My diminishing eyesight and the desire to learn instinctive shooting led me to Plains, Montana. Plains is a long way from San Antonio where I began my police training; and 2016 is a long time from 1979. In case you don't feel like doing the math, it's just over 1524 miles between the locations as the crow flies and 37 years between the decades. For nearly four decades I trained, shot, and was very confident in my marksmanship ability with firearms, especially the handgun.

Why Plains, Montana? Doug Dryden of Highlands Tactical. A friend of mine suggested I contact Doug about doing church security training. Before calling Doug I took a look at his website (highlandstactical.com). Highlands Tactical's philosophy for instinctive shooting intrigued me,

"The goal of our courses is to teach the fundamental principles of instinctive, threat focused shooting."[103] After looking at the website I contacted Doug. I needed to learn more about what has been dubbed *combat shooting*.

> *"The goal of our courses is to teach the fundamental principles of instinctive, threat focused shooting."*
> –Highland Tactical

Combat shooting

During our initial phone conversation, Doug's passion for properly training police officers and law-abiding citizens to win a gunfight was evident. Doug is a deputy with the Sanders County, MT, Sheriff's Office and has worked as a game warden, a Director of Corporate Security for an international company, and a Tactical Security Consultant. Doug and his instructors have taught tactical handgun and carbine courses for years.

In earlier chapters I discussed the necessity of Reality Based Training (RBT) to prepare mentally for a gunfight. In addition to fear induced scenario training with nonlethal training aids, it is essential to be trained in combat shooting. The terms point shooting, instinctive shooting, combat shooting, and tactical shooting are used interchangeably in this book. Simply stated, they mean shooting the object you are looking at without thinking about stance, grip, sight alignment, sight picture, trigger control, breathing, and follow through. It means focusing on your target, not your front sight. The most descriptive is "instinctive shooting." My first introduction to instinctive shooting was with a slingshot.

Working "mids" (the 10 pm to 6 am shift) in the Air Force on a rather secure military base left young airmen

---

[103] (Dryden, 2015)

bored and sleepy. To help pass the time and stay awake I picked up a slingshot. When stuck on gate-duty at about 2 or 3 am, I'd set up some cans and plink at them with my new toy. Naturally, I used the shooting fundamentals I picked up in firearms training. I tried placing the target evenly between the slingshot's two posts, closing one eye, controlling my breathing, etc. Occasionally I'd get a hit, but for the most part my shots missed. One early morning my sergeant came by to check in with me. Seeing my slingshot, he asked if he could give it a try (I'd seen him shoot to qualify—I wasn't expecting much). "Sure" I told him. To my amazement, he consistently hit the cans. "How do you do it?" I asked. "Instinct" he said. "When I was in the P.I. [Philippine Islands] the native Philippines taught me to use one. Just look at your target and shoot." Sounded simple, just point and shoot. I gave it a try and was startled to discover that I was hitting the target more often than missing it. I also found out that the more "thinking" about shooting I did the more I missed.

> *The goal of combat shooting "is to get a disabling hit upon your opponent before he can do the same to you, regardless of how you go about it."*
> —Bill Jordan

As discussed above, the goal of marksmanship shooting is to shoot as accurately as possible to achieve a tight group and high score. Jordan says the goal of combat shooting "is to get a disabling hit upon your opponent before he can do the same to you, regardless of how you go about it."[104] Dryden articulates his training goal similarly: "The goal of instinctive shooting is to obtain acceptable accuracy (sometimes called combat accuracy) while shooting rapidly. Students are taught to balance speed

---

[104] (Jordan, 1965, p. 91)

and accuracy while center mass shooting as opposed to target shooting."[105]

Gunfights can take place inside, outside, in open areas with no cover or concealment, to the closed quarters of a vehicle. There is no one specific form or method of combat shooting because every gunfight is different. Bill Jordan in his book *No Second Place Winner* advocated point shooting or instinctive shooting, and he says the nature of combat shooting is governed by the situation. However, Jordan says the greatest single factor is *range* (the distance you are from the assailant) the second is *speed* (the time you have to respond).[106] The *distance* dictates the *speed.* The closer your opponent is the faster your reaction must be. Conversely, as the range increases the more time you have to use the gun sights and obtain proper sight alignment.

According to the Highlands Tactical website,

> Students are taught to first allow their eyes to focus on a threat or specific area of a threat, recognizing that their hands will subconsciously align the weapon to where the focus of the eye is. Learning proper trigger control (trigger weld) then makes for very accurate rapid shooting.

> Students are taught to work with their body's natural response (gross motor skills) when they experience an "adrenaline dump" in a dangerous or critical incident as opposed to trying to use fine or complex motor skills. [107]

---

[105] (Dryden, 2015)
[106] (Jordan, 1965, p. 91)
[107] (Dryden, 2015)

Sounds an awful lot like the slingshot lesson I was given years ago. Which is fine. But does it work for handgun shooting under stress? If it does work, how much training does it require? Can the average person be trained to quickly and consistently hit a "reasonable sized" target without an excessive amount of training? Seeking answers to these questions, I signed up for Highlands Tactical's 8-hour "Instinctive Self-Defense Handgun 1" course.

The course was scheduled for a Saturday and Doug invited me to drive up Friday from my home in Idaho Falls, Idaho. He claimed Sanders County is the prettiest county in Montana. I haven't been everywhere in Montana, but I've seen enough to know that was a big claim. Turning west off highway 93 onto highway 200 and into Sanders County I soon realized Doug could make a good argument for his claim. For several miles Highway 200 parallels the Flathead River as it weaves through the pine covered Cabinet Mountains rising up on either side of it. One thing I noticed that Sanders County lacked was people. The population of the nearly 2,800 square miles of the county is just over 11,000. That figures to be less than four people for every square mile.

Doug, his wife, and youngest daughter welcomed me into their home nestled against a national forest and over-looking a gorgeous valley where the Flathead meanders by. Like any two red-blooded American law enforcement officers would, we talked family, faith, and firearms into the evening. The passion that I heard in Doug's voice over the phone for training men and women to win gunfights was confirmed in person. Like a child on Christmas Eve, I couldn't wait for Saturday and a day at the range.

The first hour we spent in the classroom where Doug emphasized safety and his three principles to achieve quick and accurate shots without using sights. Doug emphasized that instinctive shooting without sights is only for close quarters. Marksmanship skills become more important as the distance between you and a threat increases—I noticed all of Doug's guns still had sights on them!

Doug, a skilled teacher, understands there are a limited number of things students are able to grasp, master, and duplicate in a high-stress situation. Hence, rather than attempt to teach students the proper stance, grip, sight alignment, sight picture, trigger control, breathing, and follow through he keeps his teaching to three basic principles. So, what about all those basic marksmanship fundamentals? Is Doug advocating an entirely new approach of controlling and discharging a lethal weapon? Let's take a look.

Stance. Important to remember is that the body will naturally have certain responses when threatened. Doug does not emphasize a marksman's shooting stance for this reason. A normal response to a physical threat is to crouch and step away from a threat. Rather than fight this, Doug uses this in his training. Further, gunfights don't always take place from a standing position. You may have to draw and fire from inside a vehicle, sitting in a chair, laying on the ground, running toward a threat, or while seeking cover or concealment. Hence, shooting from a proper marksmanship stance quickly loses importance in a gunfight.

Sight alignment and sight picture. Sight alignment and a sight picture, in the traditional understanding of these two aspects of marksmanship shooting, are obviously not used in point shooting. That being said, we come to understand that when the gun naturally points where the eyes are focused a sight picture of naturally looking over the top of the gun takes place.

Breathing. Breath control is important for distance shooting and when seeking precise shots, but not in close-quarter combat shooting. Besides, we know breathing is going to naturally take place, in a gunfight you won't think about cutting off your breath and holding it to steady the gun (see the discussion about tactical breathing in the discussion about Condition Black). This leaves three fundamentals: grip, trigger control, and follow through.

Grip, trigger control, and follow through. Doug melds these three fundamentals into his second principle. The three principles he teaches are:

1. Believe in yourself, your hands will go to where your eye is focused.
2. Trigger control—utilizing the trigger reset.
3. Look first, move the head, settle your eye on a specific spot. The hand will stop where the eye is focused.

The first principle, *"Believe in yourself, your hands will go to where your eye is focused"* isn't something you have to remember in a gunfight, it's a principle to understand for training and one you will *know* is true when you leave the range. To make his point that *your hands will go where your eyes are focused* Doug used a baseball analogy. Anybody who has ever played organized baseball or softball can hear the coach saying, "Keep your eye on the ball." Simple. Being a former Little League Baseball® coach I got it. The other coaches and I would tell the players to, "Watch the ball into the glove" and to, "Watch the ball all the way to the bat." I've never seen sights on a baseball glove or bat. Your hands just naturally go where your eyes are focused. Makes sense. In a gunfight this principle means you shoot where you are looking. This is why it's common for people involved in a shooting to shoot the gun of their adversary—that is what they were looking at. If that's what we do naturally, and can hit what we are looking at, why would we teach students to focus on something else?

The second principle, *"Trigger control utilizing the trigger reset"* is a combination of having a proper grip, trigger press, reset, and follow through. Semi-automatic pistols generally have a short trigger reset. After a shot is fired a semi-automatic pistol will cycle and load another round into the chamber readying the gun to be fired again—that's the *automatic* part. However, the trigger needs to be reset by the shooter—that's the *semi* part. When the shooter's trigger finger releases the trigger to move forward it will reset the firing mechanism and allow for another shot. Almost without fail, every shooter will completely release his or her finger as far as the trigger guard will allow and then reengage the trigger for a follow-up shot. It is unnecessary to completely release the trigger and doing so sacrifices time and accuracy. The trigger only needs to be let out enough to reset. By doing this you maintain your grip and can quickly shoot an accurate follow-up shot.

The third principle, *"Look first, move the head, settle your eye on a specific spot. The hand will stop where the eye is focused"* is based on the first principle that your hands will go where your eyes are focused. Doug teaches to pick out a spot on your target, concentrate on that spot, point, and shoot. On a human target this may be a button, a design, or spot on a shirt or coat. This principle is critical when facing multiple targets and/or shooting while moving. Rather than moving the gun and your eyes at the same time, "Look first" calls you to pick out your spot, then move your gun and take your shot. Properly executed this will prevent over-travel and shooting to the side of your intended target.

Simply put these principles can be summed up as: (1) *trust your body to do the right thing,* (2) *get and maintain a proper grip—pay attention to trigger reset,* and (3) *look first.* Okay does it work? We went to the range.

We started out at the two-yard line. Our targets were white cardboard silhouette targets (18" x 30"). With his Sharpie® Doug placed a quarter-sized black dot in the middle of each target, giving each shooter a point of focus. He had us get in a crouched position—the position your body will naturally go to when threatened. For the first several strings of fire we began by holding our guns close to our chest in the safety circle position described in chapter eight. When told to shoot we punched our guns straight out, holding them chest high, keeping our eyes focused on the dot and looking over the top of our guns. There were six of us in the class, and all of us shot amazingly well. For the most part, that was it. No tricks. No secrets. Just straightforward practical principles: ensure you have a proper grip; look at your target; point at it; and shoot.

Doug and his son, Ben, instintive shooting. Note how Ben is looking over the gun sights. He is looking at what he wants to shoot.

Doug added to the drill throughout the day. Shooting multiple targets, moving and shooting, shooting while moving, shooting from closer and further distances (from one to eight yards). As our skills increased our targets multiplied, the distances increased, and Doug pushed for faster times. But the basics remained: have a proper grip; look at your target; point at it; and shoot. After shooting a couple hundred rounds it became apparent the "one thing" to remember is to "look first." Look first, pick out a small target, point, and shoot. Before the end of the day I was able to shoot 15 rounds, with two-reloads (3 magazines, 5 rounds each), while moving from side to side and backwards, in under 10 seconds without missing a center-mass shot.

The two of us in class with prior police training occasionally needed to be reminded to keep our guns chest high as we had a tendency to raise them to eye level. As we progressed throughout the day shooting became more instinctive. Rather than thinking "front sight" I was concentrating on the target. That's what you'll do in a gunfight. You will not be thinking "front sight," your focus will be on the threat before you. It is this reality that leads Doug to stress "good shots" and not "tight groups." Three shots in a 5 inch group are just as effective at eliminating a threat as 3 shots in a 1 inch group. And those shots are even more effective when they can be fired before a threat has the chance to shoot you.

In less than three hours and with only 200 rounds my questions were answered. Yes, instinctive shooting works for handgun shooting under stress. To get the basics down it doesn't take long. Learning to shoot instinctively takes less time than marksmanship training. And finally, the average person can absolutely be trained to quickly and consistently hit a "reasonable sized" target without an excessive amount of training.

Equipment

Chapter 10

Miami FBI Shooting

In 1986 the Miami area was hit with a slew of bank robberies and a special Federal Bureau of Investigation (FBI) task force was assigned to the case. On April 11, 1986, eight FBI agents were involved in a gunfight that would, among other things, result in a change of FBI and law enforcement equipment.

The two bank robbers, William Matix and Michael Platt, were in a black Monte Carlo driven by Matix. The suspects were being followed by FBI agents Ben Grogan and Jerry Dove. Six other agents (in four other vehicles) were also following Matix and Platt. The decision was made to stop the suspects by forcing them off the road and blocking any escape route. The agents rammed into the Monte Carlo forcing it into the small parking lot of 12201 82nd Avenue in south Dade County. The suspects' vehicle was squeezed between a parked Oldsmobile Cutlass on their right and Agent Dick Manauzzi's car on their left. Grogan and Dove's car stopped about 20 feet behind the Monte Carlo. Supervisor Agent Gordon McNeill stopped his car perpendicular to and at the rear of Manauzzi's car (see figure 10-1).

131

As soon as the cars came to a stop gunfire erupted. Platt, armed with a Ruger mini-14, semi-automatic .223 caliber rifle starting shooting at Manauzzi. Unfortunately, during the car pursuit Manauzzi had placed his revolver on the seat between his legs for easier access. But, to stop the suspects he had to ram their vehicle twice, which caused his driver's door to pop open. During the impact, Manauzzi's gun slid from the seat and he believed it tumbled into the street. When Platt opened up on him, the agent quickly ran

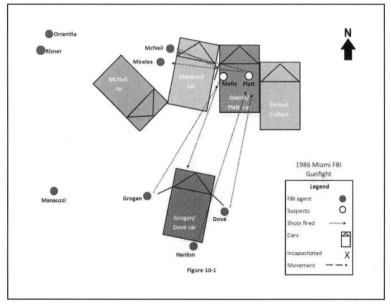

Figure 10-1

from his car and retreated to search for his lost revolver. Even though Platt fired several shots at Manauzzi's car, he was unable to get a clean shot at the agent. However, Manauzzi was hit with bullet fragments.

While Platt was shooting at Manauzzi, Matix opened his driver's door the few inches he was able, and fired a shot towards Grogan and Dove with a 12-gauge shotgun loaded with #6 birdshot. From 25 feet behind the Monte Carlo, they returned fire with their Smith and Wesson 9mm pistols.

Grogan hit Matix in the right forearm. The 9mm, 115 grain jacketed hollow point bullet traveled completely through Matix's right forearm, causing minimal injury.

Meanwhile, agents McNeill and Ed Mireles rushed to the front left fender of Manauzzi's car and immediately began taking fire from Platt. Mireles, armed with a Remington 870 12-gauge shotgun loaded with 00 buckshot, was hit in the left forearm from Platt's .223 and knocked down before he could get a shot off. Mireles was unable to use his left arm for the remainder of the gunfight. McNeill emptied his six shot revolver—a Smith and Wesson .357, loaded with .38+P hollow points—into the Monte Carlo and hit Matix at least twice. McNeill's fifth shot entered on the right side of Matix's head, just in front of his ear. The bullet came to rest in his maxillary sinus cavity. Dr. W. French Anderson believes this rendered Matix unconscious.[108] The injury caused Matix to slump down facing McNeill. McNeill's sixth shot entered the right side of Matix's neck, hit the bulk of neck muscles connected to the spinal cord, traveled downward and came to rest on top of (after hitting, but not puncturing) his right lung.[109] Matix was temporarily out of the fight.

Platt exited through the passenger window of the Monte Carlo while Dove continued to fire at him from the rear. Agents Gil Orrantia and Ron Risner, who were across the street and to the left and front of the Monte Carlo, were also shooting at Platt. In order to exit the Monte Carlo, Platt had to climb out the passenger window and on to the hood of the parked Cutlass. The exposed Platt was hit four times exiting the car. One shot from Dove's 9mm passed through his upper right arm, into his chest cavity, and into his right lung. A second bullet from Dove passed through his left foot from left to right. A third bullet was a through-and-through

---

[108] (Anderson, 2006, p. 25)
[109] (Anderson, 2006, p. 26)

wound of Platt's upper right thigh. A fourth bullet (from either Dove or Orrantia) scraped across his back causing an abrasion.

After exiting the Monte Carlo, Platt again shot at McNeill and Mireles. Both agents went down. McNeill took a shot to his neck that rendered him out of the fight and parallelized for several hours. Platt then rushed the agents located behind the Monte Carlo. Agent John Hanlon had joined Dove and Grogan taking a position at the rear of the Grogan/Dove car. All three agents were shot and went to the ground. Platt shot Dove and Grogan at point blank range, killing both agents. Hanlon was shot in the hand and groin, taking him out of the fight (see figure 10-2).

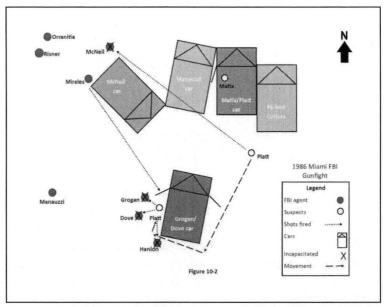

Figure 10-2

Unbelievably, Matix regained consciousness, exited the Monte Carlo and joined Platt at the Grogan/Dove car. Although Mireles was seriously injured, he worked the pump-action shotgun with one hand and was able to shoot at Platt from a sitting position behind McNeill's car. Platt took several hits from the buckshot, but continued to move and get into the driver's seat of the Grogan/Dove car. Matix got into the passenger seat. Platt, with an injured right arm attempted to start the car with his left hand, while Mireles continued to fire the shotgun until it was empty. Pulling himself up, Mireles, drew his Smith and Wesson .357 magnum—loaded with six rounds of .38 +P—and staggered towards the car with the suspects inside. Mireles shot all six rounds into the car hitting Platt once in the head and once in the chest, and Matix three times in the head. With both suspects finally incapacitated, the gunfight was over (see figure 10-3).

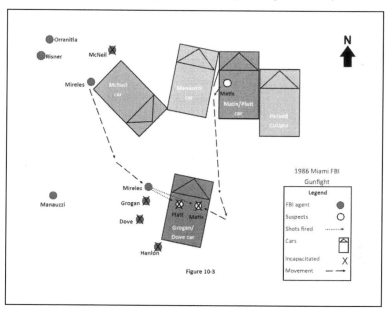

Figure 10-3

The gun battle left both suspects and two FBI agents (Grogan and Dove) dead. Agents Mireles, McNeill, and Hanlon sustained serious injuries. Agents Manauzzi and Orrantia received minor injuries. Agent Risner survived unscathed. There were 49 verified shots fired by the suspects and 70 verified shots by the agents.[110] During the gunfight

---

[110] (Anderson, 2006, p. 13)

Platt received 12 gunshot wounds and Matix six. For a detailed account of the shooting see *Forensic Analysis of the April 11, 1986, FBI Firefight* by Dr. W. French Anderson.

This Miami FBI shooting has been analyzed and scrutinized by federal, state, local, and private police trainers. While there's a lot to be learned about how much trauma a human could take and remain in the fight, one of the biggest outcomes directly associated with this gunfight was the development of the .40 caliber bullet. As in the Newhall shooting, the FBI agents were out gunned by the felons.

The weapons used by the suspects are as follows: Matix was armed with a 12-gauge shotgun (1 round fired). Platt used a .223 caliber rifle (42 rounds fired) and two .357 magnum revolvers (3 rounds fired from each gun). Seven of the eight FBI agents on scene fired shots. The agents were armed as follows: McNeill (6 rounds fired) and Orrantia (12 rounds fired) each had a .357 magnum revolvers loaded with 38+P; Mireles used a 12-gauge shotgun loaded with 00 buckshot (5 rounds fired) and a .357 magnum revolver loaded with 38+P (6 rounds fired); Grogan (9 rounds fired), Dove (20 rounds fired), and Risner (at least 13-14 rounds fired) all used 9mm semi-automatics loaded with 115 grain jacketed hollow point bullets. Risner also fired one round from a .38 revolver loaded with .38 +P. Hanlon (5 rounds fired) used a .38 revolver loaded with .38 +P.[111]

The two largest issues coming out of the incident were (1) Platt inflicted devastating wounds with his rifle; and (2) despite receiving several gunshot wounds, some even fatal, both suspects were able to remain in the fight for several minutes. Following this shooting, officers began to doubt their equipment and question the effectiveness of the 9mm bullet to stop an aggressor. The fact is, you must not only be trained and prepared to use your equipment, you must also

---

[111] (Anderson, 2006, p. 13)

be confident *in* your equipment. For years the Fram® company marketed their more expensive oil filters by claiming the quality of protection was worth the price. The tagline for their commercials was, "You can pay me now, or pay me later." Quality does make a difference—especially when it comes to handguns, holsters, and ammunition. However, as with most things, quality does not necessarily mean the most expensive. Remember, your goal in a gunfight isn't to kill, but to stop the aggressor from killing or attempting to kill. Therefore, you want equipment best suited for stopping quickly and effectively.

Ammunition

Enormous improvement in ballistics has been made since the FBI shooting. This is especially important since the most critical piece of equipment in a gunfight is the bullet. The bullet, which comes in different sizes and weights, is the projectile that comes out of the barrel. The terms "cartridge" and "round" refer collectively to the bullet, case, primer, and gunpowder. Short of the aggressor giving up, it's the bullet that does the stopping.

The effectiveness of a bullet depends on the transfer of kinetic energy from the moving bullet to the object hit by the bullet. The speed or velocity of the bullet determines its kinetic energy. The faster the bullet, the more energy it has available to transfer. A car traveling 70 mph is going to do more damage than the same car traveling 5 mph. The same is true with bullets. It's not the bullet itself; it's the energy of the bullet that's created by its speed. Kinetic energy is proportional to the square of its velocity.[112] Kinetic energy is created by the motion of an object, so the faster the speed the more kinetic energy. That's why the lighter 55 to 77 grain rifle bullets shot from Platt's .223 caliber rifle were far more

---

[112] (The Physics Classroom, 1996-2015)

devastating than the 9mm 115 grain pistol bullets that hit Platt. The muzzle velocity[113] of bullets from the .223 rifle was over 3,000 feet per second (fps). Whereas the 9mm bullets were traveling about 1,200 fps and the .38 +P 900 fps or less.

Velocity is more critical to kinetic energy than mass. However, mass does make a difference. A twenty-pound sledge hammer is going to do a lot more damage than a twelve-ounce finishing hammer traveling at the same speed. Using a large and fast bullet will create more kinetic energy (mass times velocity squared: $KE = mv^2$). Nevertheless, speed is more important than mass.

However, speed can be overdone. Too much speed will result in over penetration. The faster the bullet moves the more likely it will be to completely penetrate the target. This means the bullet passes into and then through its intended target. Over penetration is negative for two reasons: first, a bullet that completely penetrates a target will continue until stopped by something or someone else. Newton's first law of motion: an object in motion will remain in motion until an external force acts upon it. Second, a bullet that completely penetrates a target still has energy and any energy that isn't used to stop the aggressor is wasted energy.

Hollow point bullets were developed in an effort to prevent over penetration. A bullet that does not over penetrate means all of its kinetic energy is transferred to the object hit. Bullets are generally made out of lead, because of lead's mass and softness. Full metal jacketed bullets are (generally) lead bullets covered with a thin coat of copper. Hollow point bullets have a hole in the tip. When a hollow point bullet enters an object (i.e. a human body) the bullet is designed to open up and spread out in a mushroom shape,

---

[113] Muzzle velocity is the speed of the bullet immediately after leaving the gun barrel.

thus slowing it down like a parachute on the back of a drag racer.

Bullets fragmenting and breaking up also causes loss of effectiveness, especially if the bullet first travels through an object such as a door or glass. This was an issue in the Miami shooting. Several of the bullets recovered from Platt and Matix were fragments.[114] Bullets can also fragment after entering the body. In an effort to keep bullets in one piece, some bullet manufacturers have started bonding the outer jacket to the bullet's core. These are referred to as "bonded" bullets.

While there have been great advances in ballistics, be cautioned, there is no "magic" bullet that's guaranteed to stop a person immediately. What's the best bullet to use? First, let me caution what not to use. Never use hand-loaded ammunition (rounds that are loaded by private individuals) for "duty" ammunition. Even when using the best hand-loaded rounds there is simply too much room for error. Furthermore, in the event of a shooting the decision to use hand-loaded ammunition may have to be defended in court. Therefore, the best choice is to use the same rounds used by law enforcement. Ammunition companies manufacture cartridges specifically for law enforcement. Most police agencies do extensive studies prior to selecting ammunition. Check with local and state police agencies for their choice of ammunition. If the question comes up in court concerning the choice of ammunition you may confidently reply that it was based on what police in your area use. Police are the professionals, let them do the research and defend the selection.

As mentioned before, the most effective bullet is the fastest and biggest. Does that mean a 350 grain .500 S&W magnum traveling in excess of 1900 fps is the best choice? No, because the law of diminishing returns begins to take

---

[114] (Anderson, 2006, pp. 19-76)

effect. Too fast and too big will have too much penetration and will most likely over penetrate. Also, there's the consideration of practicality. Bigger and faster means a larger cartridge and will require a larger gun. Also, the more powerful the cartridge the bigger the recoil.

The most common calibers used by police are 9mm, .40 S&W, and .45 ACP. Ballistics for the 9mm have developed greatly in recent years. Each of these calibers are

Speer® Gold Dot® Ammunition			
Caliber	**Weight**	**MV**	**Energy**
9mm	124	1150	364
.40 S&W	165	1150	484
.45 ACP	185	1050	453

Weight: grains
MV: Muzzle Velocity fps
Energy: in foot pounds
(Source: speer-ammo.com/ballistics/ammo.aspx)
Figure 10-4

proven effective in stopping aggressors. See the chart (figure 10-4) comparing the 9mm, .40 S&W, and .45 ACP. The advantages of the 9mm are its low recoil and smaller cartridges. Low recoil means it's easier to shoot and more manageable, while small cartridges means more ammunition available. The disadvantage is the ballistic capabilities of this round are significantly less in foot pounds than the other two. While it is moving faster than the .45, its mass is much less. The .40 S&W has the best ballistics; the velocity equals the 9mm but it is 41 grains heavier. While larger than the 9mm (less rounds available), it is still smaller than the .45 ACP. The drawback to the .40 S&W is the recoil. Of the three calibers it has the most "kick" when shot. The .45 ACP is the bullet with the most mass, but is traveling the slowest. A general recommendation and popular choice by police for any of these calibers is the Gold Dot® by Speer®.

All three of the above rounds are designed for semi-automatic handguns (although they may be used in specially designed revolvers). If considering a revolver the two most

Speer® Gold Dot® Ammunition			
Caliber	**Weight**	**MV**	**Energy**
.38+P	125	945	248
.357 Mag.	125	1450	584
.44 Mag.	210	1450	980

Weight: grains
MV: Muzzle Velocity fps
Energy: in foot pounds
(Source: speer-ammo.com/ballistics/ammo.aspx)
Figure 10-5

popular calibers are the .38 Special and the .357 Magnum. In the Miami shooting three FBI agents had .357 magnums, but they were loaded with a much less powerful .38+P. Note the difference in energy between the two bullets of the same weight in figure 10-5. Included in the comparison is the .44 Magnum.

Firearms

There are a myriad of quality handguns available in today's market for a variety of purposes. Handguns are de-signed to meet the specific and very different wants of shoot-ing enthusiasts. There are handguns designed for plinking (targets that pop visually or audibly when hit, like tin cans or glass bottles), competition (from speed shooting to cowboy action shooting to silhouette target shooting), hunting, con-cealed carry, self-defense, and combat to name a few. With so many different choices, selecting a handgun for the novice shooter can be overwhelming. However, with a little infor-mation, you can quickly narrow down the selection.

Choosing a handgun, like any tool, begins with determining its purpose. Select a handgun designed for the specific application for which the gun will be used. A combat handgun will best meet the needs for police officers, security personal, and general self-defense. Combat handguns fall into two basic categories: revolver and semi-automatic. Both have benefits. The bottom line is this–anyone involved in a gunfight wants to have the most powerful gun with the most bullets. Realistically, select a handgun that you can safely and accurately shoot and can be carried comfortably concealed, (assuming you will be carrying a concealed handgun).

Revolvers

The National Rifle Association (NRA) defines a revolver as a handgun "that has a rotating cylinder containing a number of firing chambers. The action of the trigger or hammer will line up a chamber with the barrel and firing pin."[115] There are two basic types of revolvers: single-action and double-action. A single-action revolver is the old "cowboy" style that requires the hammer to be thumbed back to cock the gun. Once cocked the trigger is pulled to release the hammer and fire the gun. With the hammer cocked it doesn't take much pressure on the trigger to release the hammer, causing the gun to fire. Single action revolvers are great for plinking, hunting, or shooting in competitions such as silhouette and Cowboy Action Shooting. A single-action revolver is not recommended, and in fact, highly discouraged for self-defense and combat situations. If opting for a revolver, select a double-action revolver.

Three of the largest American gun companies (Smith and Wesson, Colt, and Ruger) all manufacture quality double-action combat revolvers and smaller revolvers made for

---

[115] (Basic Pistol Course, Natiional Rifle Association, 2009, p. I-3)

concealed carry. Unlike a single-action revolver, the hammer on a double-action revolver doesn't need to be cocked first. When the trigger is pulled the hammer cocks and then drops, causing the gun to fire. The benefit of a double-action/combat revolver over a semi-automatic is its simplicity. Revolvers are easy to learn to shoot, reliable, and rarely have malfunctions. The drawbacks are a limited number of rounds (five or six), the size and weight of full frame guns, and difficulty reloading quickly in high stress situations.

Semi-automatics

Revolvers, as good and reliable as they are, are yesterday's combat guns. Today's combat guns are semi-automatic, double-action only, striker-fire pistols. The world of handguns changed when Sam Colt invented the revolver in 1836. The next major change came when John Browning designed the .45 Automatic Pistol that was manufactured by Colt® and became known as the "1911". The 1911 pistol was issued by the US Army from 1911 to 1986, and remains a popular pistol for self-defense and sport shooting. In 1981 Austrian engineer Gaston Glock developed his "Safe Action"® pistol for the Austrian army. Catching the eye of American police, Glock's double-action only, striker-fire pistol soon became the new standard for combat pistols. As with double-action revolvers and model 1911 pistols, today nearly every major gun company makes a double-action only, striker-fire pistol.

Like single-action revolvers, single-action semi-automatic pistols perform a single action when the trigger is pulled. The drawback of single-action semi-automatic pistols (such as the 1911) is the same as single-action revolvers; they traditionally have a short and rather light trigger pull that may lead to unintentional discharges in high stress situations. They also have a positive safety that must be disengaged prior to firing. Hence, in high stress situations you

143

must remember to disengage the safety. Unless you've trained enough to create a reflexive response to disengaging the safety, chances are you will find yourself trying to discharge a locked weapon in a deadly gunfight.

The double-action only semi-automatics mimic the trigger pull of a double-action revolver, albeit with a shorter trigger pull. For police officers of the 1980s and 1990s, who were transitioning from a revolver to a semi-automatic, the double-action semi-automatic was more natural and required less training. In 1992, after carrying a Smith and Wesson revolver as a duty gun since 1979 (in both the Air Force and on the department), the San Antonio Police Department switched me to the Glock model 22. The transition from a revolver to the Glock pistol took three training days with about 700 rounds fired. In 2009 I joined the Bonneville County Sheriff's Office as a reserve deputy and was issued a Para Ordinance 1911. I had to relearn the reflexive response of disengaging a manual safety—something I had not done since the beginning of my law enforcement career. I repeatedly forgot to disengage the slide lock safety at the beginning of each shooting stage when given the command to fire. I had a tough time readjusting to the 1911, but the key is training. Remember, the more complicated the tool, the more training and repetition required.

Finally, keep in mind that whatever handgun you select, you should always ensure it is designed for combat and you must train with it to obtain a solid level of competence.

Firearm modifications

If it can be attached to a gun, labeled "tactical" and painted OD green or black it will sell in the world of firearms. The firearms industry has an ever-increasing list of accessories to modify, enhance, or add-on to handguns. The manufactures attempt to make the consumer believe the gun isn't good enough right out of the box. In order to be a better shot attachments must be added, triggers must be modified, and sights must be replaced—hogwash! That just doesn't fly in the world of combat. Perhaps this is true in handgun competitions or hunting, but in the world of combat quality handguns come ready for action. There is simply too much at stake for gun companies not to produce an out-of-the-box ready gun. Police departments purchase combat handguns by the hundreds or thousands and they expect them to be dependable with no modifications necessary—and they are.

Keep your carry firearm as simple and as close to factory specifications as possible. Most police departments forbid officers to modify their service pistols. Those that do permit alterations require that a certified armorer perform the modifications. The most important piece of equipment in a gunfight is your brain, but the second is your gun. You want it to be reliable and consistent. Your firearm becomes increasingly more complicated with the addition of modifications or special equipment. Plus, each addition carries its own set of uncontrollable factors like malfunction or user error.

That being said, there are some acceptable and popular modifications to a combat handgun such as sights, lighting systems, and grips. All combat handguns come equipped with their own sights. These are often referred to as the gun's iron sights. However, iron sights are regularly replaced by night sights. In fact, many police departments order their duty pistols with night sights from the manufacturer. Night sights are designed to provide greater sight visibility in low light situations. Generally, this modification uses a three-dot system with two dots inset in the rear sight and one dot inset in the front sight. These dots have radioactive isotopes that cause them to "glow" in low and no-light environments. Trijicon® makes night sights for all popular combat pistols. They run about $125 for a set plus the necessary cost of a gunsmith mounting them. Besides night sights, laser sights are an acceptable and popular modification. They even come standard on some of today's pistols. However, laser sights should never be used to teach someone how to shoot. Laser sights should only supplement a proper sight picture. Under high stress conditions it's easier to pick up your firearm's front sight than to look for a small laser bouncing around off a moving and mobile target. Because of this, laser sights should not be relied upon for combat use. Perhaps the best aftermarket optics becoming popular today are see-through, low-profile, micro reflex sights that allow the shooter to use either enhanced optics or the gun's iron sights. The pricey, but quality Smith and Wesson® M&P C.O.R.E (Competition Optics Ready Equipment) 9mm comes ready for mounting one of these high-priced optics. This modification could very well be the wave of the future for police.

Lighting systems are the other acceptable and popular addition. This modification places a small, tactical use only light onto your firearm. Where the laser sight provides bullet placement precision, the gun-mounted light provides whole target illumination. However, a gun-mounted light should only be supplemental to a hand-held flashlight. There's too big a temptation to use the gun as a flashlight. Recall the second cardinal rule of firearms safety—*never point your muzzle at anything you're not willing to destroy*. Therefore, if you train with lights I recommend becoming skilled using handheld flashlights and only use gun-mounted lights as supplements when the gun will be pointed exclusively at the threat.

Finally, aftermarket grips for some models are also popular and easy to install. Grips of various sizes and textures are available. Larger or smaller grips will help you to have a proper and consistent hold on the gun. Rubberized grips can provide a more secure hold and comfortable fit and thereby decrease the chances of hand fatigue. However, avoid grips, holsters, or any other add-on item that features images or writing that may be misinterpreted by a jury. Remember, in the event of a shooting, your handgun will be confiscated for evidence and presented to the jury in the event of a trial. You probably don't want to have a skull and crossbones, the "Grim Reaper" or "Zombie Hunter" etched into the side of your gun.

Holsters

Every handgun should be carried in a holster that is specifically designed for that handgun. The holster should protect the trigger from being unintentionally pulled and should securely hold the handgun in place. Just like selecting a gun, you must think about combat when selecting a holster. A good combat holster will allow you to have a proper grip while the gun is still holstered. It must be both safe and comfortable. If the holster is uncomfortable or causes fatigue, then you might be tempted to carry without it. I highly discourage anyone from carrying a gun without a good quality holster designed specifically for their firearm. Many people like to carry a handgun in their waistband, inside a tucked-in shirt. While concealed and secure, this makes it difficult to draw and quickly get into a gunfight. Others like to carry a handgun inside their waistband with a tucked-in shirt. While this may feel secure, and it does conceal your weapon, it is a dangerous practice. You are far more likely to accidentally discharge your firearm without proper trigger protection. Also, holsters secure your firearm to your body so they do not slip or shift. This makes gripping and handling them far safer in the event of a genuine threat.

Many holsters are made from soft nylon material and are designed simply to carry a handgun securely and safely; but they are not designed to draw from in a combat situation. Other holsters are competition holsters designed specifically for quick draw, but lack safety features. Holsters made from leather are good, but need to be "broken in" and stretch over time. Fobus® and Blackhawk® make quality combat holsters designed specifically for plain clothes or concealed carry. These holsters are made from durable molded material that secures the gun and allows for a quick draw.

The bottom line is quality equipment that is simple to use. Invest your money wisely, your life is on the line.

A Parting Word

Chapter 11

Two days after the Orlando massacre on June 12, 2016, I came across a nationally obscure story of a gunfight. The Associated Press's reporting was simple and direct. The story's title captured the essence of the story, "Alabama police officer shoots, kills man at traffic stop." The short narrative provided a few more details:

> MOBILE, Ala. – An Alabama police officer has shot and killed an 18-year-old man during a traffic stop. Mobile Police Chief James Barber tells media outlets that an officer saw a vehicle cut off another car Monday evening. The officer stopped the vehicle, carrying driver Michael Moore and two passengers.
>
> Barber says Moore had no driver's license and was asked to step out of the car. At that point, police say the officer noticed that Moore had a gun in his waistband and reached for it. Barber says the officer shot Moore four times. He was later pronounced dead at USA Medical Center.

Barber says investigators recovered a semi-automatic .40-caliber Smith and Wesson and a magazine from the scene. The officer involved has been placed on administrative duty pending results of the investigation.

That's all there was to the story. Good guy (or gal) with a gun kills bad guy with a gun; period, end of story. But is that all there is to it? Having read this book, you know that's not all there is to it. The officer survived, but did the officer win? Winning involves winning with the body, soul, and spirit. In the first chapter we learned that in a gunfight all three are involved, and it's important to keep in mind that each one of the three aspects impact the other two. Our spirit gives us a sense of right and wrong; it's our ethical part. Our soul gives us our mental capacities; it's our intellect and where we make decisions about which specific actions to take. With the body we take action based on the decision made.

Spirit ⟶ Soul ⟶ Body

Proper preparation demands the spirit (ethical) be prepared first, followed by the soul (mental), and then the body (tactical). In the aftermath of a gunfight winning is revealed in reverse order. It's immediately apparent if the body is physically wounded. The investigation(s) by authorities in the days and weeks afterward will reveal if the soul—the decision to pull the trigger—was right.

The officer will be required to answer the questions of his agency and other authorities. He will be expected to answer the questions of friends, relatives, and co-workers. He will have to deal with the fact that he pulled the trigger and the life of another human being came to an end.

Firearms and tactic instructors will help you prepare tactically to use cover and concealment and place a good shot on your target. Reality Based Training, shooting simulators, and other decision-making training scenarios will help prepare your split-second decision making ability at the moment of truth. This preparation will help you win physically and legally. But what about spiritually?

Your spirit will inform you if you acted right. After a gunfight you will evaluate your actions. There will be no one else around. It will just be you. Your justification—*or the lack of it*—will be revealed in the deep recesses of your heart. Having a clear picture of what those ethics are today is essential for fighting off the doubts later.

Preparing spiritually will determine how (and if) you recover spiritually. Hence, prepare first by determining if you *can* pull the trigger on another human being. Be sure you are justified in your decision to use lethal force based on the facts *as you understood them* at the time of the shooting. Avoid getting caught up in false guilt. Also, keep in mind the five basic stages to killing: (1) the concern stage, (2) the actual kill, (3) exhilaration, (4) remorse, and (5) rationalization and acceptance. The last three come into play after the gunfight is over.

I mentioned in chapter two, but it bears repeating here, there is no moral or ethical prohibition against using deadly force by either the God of the Bible or Western civilization's laws and values. If you have questions or concerns about the incident talk to clergy or another trained professional.

The purpose of this book is to teach you how to win a gunfight—not merely how to survive it. My prayer is that I've accomplished that goal. If you ever have to face a moment of truth when someone threatens you or another with serious bodily injury or death make sure you're prepared ethically, mentally, and tactically. Make sure your spirit, soul, and body are ready. Should we seek peace? Absolutely, as a

151

Christian I agree with the biblical mandate, *"If possible, so far as it depends on you, live peaceably with all."*[116] But, there may come a time when you are not able to live at peace and find yourself in a gunfight. Prepare now to win.

---

[116] (Romans 12:18)

Epilogue

Winning—in the End

This book has been about winning—winning a gunfight. But even more important than winning a gunfight is winning in life. I've contended that each person is made up of three parts: a spirit, a soul, and a body.

When I was a homicide detective I made routine trips to the county morgue. In the morgue was a large walk-in cooler where bodies were kept awaiting an autopsy. Sometimes there were upwards of twenty bodies needing to be examined. Some were victims of homicide. Some died by accident. Some ended their own life. Some causes of death had yet to be determined. Before the autopsy all clothing and jewelry were removed. Stripped of all earthly possessions—in the same cold room, lying side-by-side, each body occupying space on a stainless steel table. Some young. Some old. Some black. Some white. Some Hispanic. Some other. Some had been rich. Some had been poor. Some had been respected by the community. Some had been imprisoned by the community. Some left behind grieving loved ones. Some left no one. But in the morgue they were all equal. There was no distinction. Each body was alike. All were the same. Death is the great equalizer. All humanity stands equal before God. Equal how?

Equal in guilt, *"For all have sinned and fall short of the glory of God"* (Romans 3:23). In God's eyes we are all equal—equally guilty. *"None is righteous, no not one"* (Romans 3:10). Every human is marked by sin. Every one of us is guilty. Every one of us stands condemned before a holy God—*"For there is no distinction"* (Romans 3:22). None of us will be able to go to our deathbed free of even one bad choice, having only entertained pure thoughts and motives, and living with integrity in every second of every day. *"For all have sinned"* therefore all are guilty.

Guilt—sin—falling short, all words that convey bad news. So what's the *good news*? The good news is we can be, *"justified [acquitted of all guilt] by his grace as a gift"* (Romans 3:24a). Justification is a gift. God's justification is a gift given by his grace. *"Justified"* is not to be "made guilt-less", nor is it to be "freed from the punishment due for our guilt." It is a judicial action given by God declaring a sinner righteous or "in right standing with God."

How is a sinner declared righteous by a holy God? *"Through the redemption that is in Christ Jesus"* (Romans 3:24b). Redemption was a payment to free a slave. Sinners are in bondage, or slaves, to sin. We are under the power and punishment of sin. A sinner is declared righteous by a judicial action given by God's grace in Jesus Christ, who lived a perfectly sinless life on our behalf. Faith is the mode of salvation. Christ is the means of salvation. It is Christ who redeems us. He is the payment for our redemption. His is the righteousness of which we are in such desperate need. When his payment and perfection are accredited to our account by faith in him we are justly forgiven by God (Matthew 26:28).

This declaration of righteousness occurs at the moment we believe Christ effectively paid the ransom that our sin demanded and rose from the dead to conquer sin and death, respectfully (Romans 10:9-10). When a sinner puts his or her faith in Jesus Christ they are declared righteous. How did Jesus effect the righteousness of God? By his sacrificial death, *"whom God put forward as a propitiation by his blood, to be received by faith"* (Romans 3:25a). The strange word Paul uses here translated as *propitiation*, (some Bibles use *atonement* or *sacrifice*) simply means the death of Jesus on the cross was a sufficient and acceptable payment for sin.

154

This is how one ultimately wins in life, by putting his or her life in Christ. *"For 'everyone who calls on the name of the Lord will be saved'"* (Romans 10:13).

Appendix A

The New FBI Qualification Course

- Target used is the QIT-99
- Course consists of a total of 60 rounds
- Each round counts as one point
- Any hits inside the target area count
- You must draw from concealment for every string of shots
- Passing score for Agents is 48 out of 60

Stage 1: 3 yard line

- 3 rounds in 3 seconds using your strong hand only
- 3 rounds in 3 seconds using your strong hand only
- 3 rounds using strong hand only, switch hands, 3 rounds using support hand only all in 8 seconds

Total of 12 rounds for Stage 1

Stage 2: 5 yard line

From here on out, all shooting is done with two hands

- 3 rounds in 3 seconds
- 3 rounds in 3 seconds
- 3 rounds in 3 seconds
- 3 rounds in 3 seconds

Total of 12 rounds for Stage 2

Stage 3: 7 yard line

- 4 rounds in 4 seconds
- 4 rounds in 4 seconds

- Have two magazines loaded with four rounds each. Fire four rounds, reload, fire another four rounds in 8 seconds.

Total of 16 rounds for Stage 3

Stage 4: 15 yard line

- 3 rounds in 6 seconds
- 3 rounds in 6 seconds
- 4 rounds in 8 seconds

Total of 10 rounds for Stage 4

Stage 5: 25 yard line

This stage involves the use of a barricade/cover)

- Move to cover and fire 2 rounds standing, then 3 rounds kneeling all in 15 seconds
- Move to cover and fire 2 rounds standing, then 3 rounds kneeling all in 15 seconds

Total of 10 rounds for Stage 5

(Source: USA Carry, http://www.usacarry.com/new-fbi-qualification-course/, accessed December 12, 2015).

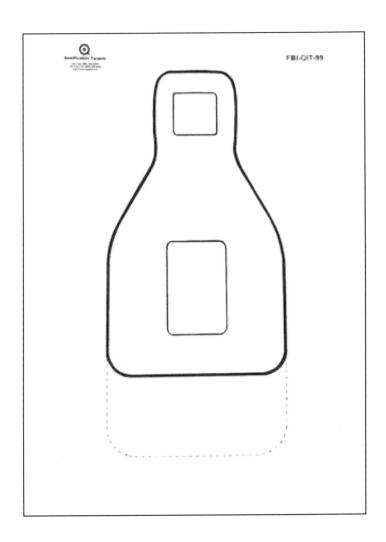

Works Cited

Anderson, W. F. (2006). *Forensic Analysis.* Boulder: Paladin Press.

Artwohl, A. (2002, October). Perceptual and Memory Distortion During Officer-Involved Shootings. *FBI Law Enforcement Bulletin*, 18-24.

Basic Pistol Course, National Rifle Association. (2009). *NRA Basic Pistol Shooting Course.* Fairfax, VA: NRA Training Department.

Biblical Studies Press, L.L.C. (1996-2006). *Holy Bible, New English Translation.* Richardson: Biblical Studies Press, L.L.C.

Blue Letter Bible. (n.d.). Retrieved from http://www.blueletterbible.org/index.cfm

Bonneville County Sheriff's Office. (2013). Active Shooter Training. Idaho Falls, ID, USA.

Brotherhood Mutual. (2015). *Brotherhood Mutual Insurance Company*. Retrieved December 28, 2015, from Safety Library, Church and Armed Security Guards: http://www.brotherhoodmutual.com/index.cfm/r esources/ministry-safety/article/should-churches-have-armed-security-guards/

Cable News Network. (2015, October 2). *CNN News*. Retrieved December 5, 2015, from Oregon shooting: Gunman dead after college rampage: http://www.cnn.com/2015/10/01/us/oregon-college-shooting/index.html

Carson, D. (1991). *Pillar New Testament Commentary, John.* Grand Rapids: Wm. B. Eerdmans Publishing Company.

Carter, J. A., Maher, S., & and Neumann, P. R. (2014). *#Greenbirds: Measuring Importance and Influence in Syrian Foreign Fighter Networks.* London: The International Centre for the Study of Radicalisation and Political Violence.

Chinn, C. (2012). *Evil Invades Sancuary.* Carl Chinn.

Chinn, C. (2016). *Ministry Violence Statistics.* Retrieved from Security? In Church?: http://www.carlchinn.com/Church_Security_Concepts.html

Cooper, J. (1972). *Principles of Personal Defense.* Boulder: Paladin Press.

Dobson, J. (2016). *Voyaging Through Life's Transitions: Guilt the Painful Emotion.* Retrieved from James Dobson's Family Talk: http://www.drjamesdobson.org/articles/voyage/guilt-the-painful-emotion

Dryden, D. (2015). *Shooting Schools-Approach.* Retrieved from Highlands Tactical Training Group:

http://www.highlandstactical.com/shooting-schools/approach/index.php

Ellis, R., Payne, E., Perez, E., & Ford, D. (2015, June 18). *Shooting suspect in custody after Charleston church massacre*. Retrieved January 30, 2016, from Cable News Network: http://www.cnn.com/2015/06/18/us/charleston-south-carolina-shooting/index.html

ESPN Sports. (2012, 12 12). A Football Life. *Marcus Allen*. USA: ESPN.

Farlex Legal Dictionary. (N.D.). *Reasonable Person*. Retrieved from The Free Dictionary by Farlex: http://legal-dictionary.thefreedictionary.com/Reasonable+person

Farlex Partner Medical Dictionary. (2012). *The Free Dictionary*. Retrieved December 23, 2015, from Medical Dictionary: http://medical-dictionary.thefreedictionary.com/phobia

Federal Bureau of Investigation, Critical Incident Response Group. (n.d.). *Active Shooter Incidents*. Retrieved from Federal Bureau of Investigation: https://www.fbi.gov/about-us/office-of-partner-engagement/active-shooter-incidents

Federal Emergency Management Agency. (2013). *Guide for Developing High-Quality Emergency Operations Plans for Houses of Worship*. US

Department of Homeland Security. Washington: US Department of Homeland Security.

Fox News. (2016, March Monday). *U.S. Home.* Retrieved 2016, from Foxnews.com: http://www.foxnews.com/us/2016/03/07/idaho-pastor-shot-day-after-praying-at-ted-cruz-rally.html

Furguson, S. B. (1988). *The Sermon on the Mount.* Edinburgh: Banner of Truth.

Gallup. (2016). *More than 9 in10 Americans Continue to Believe in God.* Retrieved from gallup.com: http://www.gallup.com/home.aspx?g_source=logo

Gorka, S. L., & Gorka, K. C. (2015). *ISIS: The Threat to the United States.* McLean: Threat Knowledge Group.

Grossman, D. (1995). The Bullet Proof Mind audio seminar.

Grossman, D. (1996). *On Killing.* US: Back Bay Books.

Grossman, D. (2008). *On Combat.* US: Warrior Science Publications.

Guinness, O. (2003). *The Call: Finding and Fulfilling the Central Purpose in Your Life.* Nashville: W

Publishing Group, A division of Thomas Nelson, Inc.

Hanson, J. (2013, May 31). *USA Carry*. Retrieved December 12, 2015, from The New FBI Qualification Course: http://www.usacarry.com/new-fbi-qualification-course/

Hicks, M. (2016, February 6). *Feds: Dearborn Hts. man supports ISIS, planned attack*. Retrieved February 20, 2016, from The Detriot News: http://www.detroitnews.com/story/news/local/wayne-county/2016/02/05/feds-dearborn-hts-man-supports-isis-planned-attack/79906302/

International Committee of the Red Cross. (1988). *Basic rules of the Geneva Conventions and their Additional.* International Committee of the Red Cross.

Jordan, B. (1965). *No Second Place Winner.* Concord, NH, USA: Police Bookshelf.

Kernan, K. (2015, December 7). *New York Post.* Retrieved December 11, 2015, from nypost.com: http://nypost.com/2015/12/07/stephen-currys-brilliance-all-starts-with-some-imagination/

Lewinski, B. (2002, November/December). Biomechanics of Lethal Force Encounters--Officer Movements. *The Police Marksman*, pp. 19-23.

Lewinski, B. (2005, August 10). *PoliceOne.com.* Retrieved December 11, 2015, from PoliceOne.com: http://www.policeone.com/officer-shootings/articles/117909-Study-reveals-important-truths-hidden-in-the-details-of-officer-involved-shootings/

Mayo Clinic. (1998-2016). *MayoClinic.org.* Retrieved from Post-traumatic stress disorder (PTSD): http://www.mayoclinic.org/

Merriam-Webster. (2011). *Merriam-Webster.com.* Retrieved April 1, 2011, from Merriam-Webster: www.merriam-webster.com/dictionary/justified

Merriam-Webster. (2016). *Merriam-Webster Online Dictionary.* Retrieved October 23, 2015, from Dictionary: http://www.merriam-webster.com/dictionary/sanctuary

Murray, K. (2016, March 9). Personal Correspondance by email.

Murray, K. R. (2004). *Training at the Speed of Life, Vol. 1.* Gotha: Armiger Publications, Inc.

National Fire Protection Association. (2015, December 4). *Religious and funeral properties.* Retrieved from The National Fire Protection Association: http://www.nfpa.org/research/reports-and-statistics/fires-by-property-

type/assemblies/religious-and-funeral-
properties

National Fire Protection Association. (2015,
December 4). *School fires with 10 or more
deaths*. Retrieved from The National Fire
Protection Association:
http://www.nfpa.org/research/reports-and-
statistics/fires-by-property-
type/educational/school-fires-with-10-or-more-
deaths

Nelson's New Illustrated Bible Dictionary. (1995).
Nelson's New Illustrated Bible Dictionary. (R. F.
Youngblood, Ed.) Nashville, TN, USA: Thomas
Nelson Pulishers.

News 12 KXII staff reporters. (2005, August 31).
Church Shootings - 911 Call For Help.
Retrieved December 5, 2015, from KXII.com:
http://www.kxii.com/home/headlines/1709036.h
tml

Police Executive Research Forum. (2014). *The Police
Response to Active Shooter Incidents.*
Washington: Police Executive Research
Forum.

Rainer, T. (2015, December 16). *16 Trends in
American Churches in 2016 (Part 1)*. Retrieved
January 29, 2016, from CP Opinion:
http://www.christianpost.com/news/16-trends-

american-churches-2016-part-1-
152468/#JMDQgpJ0dbaHgK82.99

Steffan, M. (2013, January 30). *Christianity Today*.
Retrieved January 28, 2015, from Christianity
Today.com:
http://www.christianitytoday.com/gleanings/201
3/january/deaths-from-church-attacks-rise-36-
in-2012.html

Strauss, L. (2004, July 14). *Man A Trinity (Spirit, Soul,
Body)*. Retrieved May 6, 2016, from Bible.org:
https://bible.org/seriespage/2-man-trinity-spirit-
soul-body

Stuart, D. K. (2006). *The New American Commentary,
Exodus, Vol. 2.* B&H Publishing Group:
Nashville.

Texas State University and Federal Bureau of
Investigation. (2014). *A Study of Active
Shooter Incidents in the United States Between
2000 and 2013.* Washington: U.S. Department
of Justice.

The Editors of Encyclopædia Britannica. (2015).
Hazael, King of Damascus. Retrieved from
Encyclopedia Britannnica:
http://www.britannica.com/biography/Hazael

The Federal Bureau of Investigation. (2015).
Frequently Asked Questions. Retrieved from
FBI.gov: https://www.fbi.gov/about-us/faqs

The National Rifle Association. (2012). *Basic Personal Protection in the Home Course.* Fairfax: The National Rifle Association of America.

The Physics Classroom. (1996-2015). *Kinetic Energy.* Retrieved January 15, 2016, from The Physics Classroom: http://www.physicsclassroom.com/Class/energy/u5l1c.cfm

Therapists.com. (2016). *Fundamentals Guilt-Shame.* Retrieved from therapits.com: http://www.therapists.com/fundamentals/guilt-shame

USA Today Network and KGW Staff. (2015, October 14). *http://www.cnn.com/2015/10/01/us/oregon-college-shooting/index.html.* Retrieved December 5, 2015, from KGW.com: http://www.kgw.com/story/news/local/roseburg-college-shooting/2015/10/02/hero-shot-7-times-standing-up-roseburg-shooter/73205662/

Van Horne, P., & Riely, J. A. (2014). *Left of Bang: How the Marine Corps' Combat Hunter Program Can Save Your Life.* New York: Black Irish Entertainment, LLC.

Whitbourne, S. K. (2012, August 11). *The Definitive Guide to Guilt.* Retrieved from Psychology Today:

https://www.psychologytoday.com/blog/fulfillme
nt-any-age/201208/the-definitive-guide-guilt

Wood, M. (2013). *Newhall Shooting: A tactical analysis.* Iola, WI, USA: Gun Digest Books.

About the Author

 Tim Rupp's law enforcement career spans four decades. His father was both a career military man and pastor, so it was natural for Tim to enlist in the Air Force after graduating high school in 1979. Tim served four years active duty as an Air Force law enforcement specialist. After his enlistment, Tim joined the San Antonio Police Department (SAPD) and gave 24 years of dedicated service before retiring in 2007. During his SAPD career he worked as a patrol officer, homicide detective, patrol sergeant, sex crimes sergeant, police academy supervisor, and internal affairs sergeant-investigator. Tim certified as a police firearms instructor and supervised police firearms and tactics for several years. He continues to serve with the Bonneville County Sheriff's Office as a reserve deputy.

Before retiring from the police department, Tim was called to pastor Elm Creek Baptist Church in La Vernia, TX, just outside of San Antonio. After retiring from the police department he was called to pastor fulltime in Idaho. Tim currently serves as senior pastor at River of Life Church in Idaho Falls, teaches firearms with his son, and instructs online for Crown College. He graduated from Texas State University (Master of Science in Criminal Justice), Southwestern Baptist Theological Seminary (Master of Divinity and Master of Arts in Christian Education), and Western Seminary (Doctor of Ministry). Tim is married to Sherry and they have three children, Christina, Aaron, and Emily and five grandchildren.